JESUS AND HIS COMING

JESUS
AND HIS COMING

The Emergence of a Doctrine

JOHN A. T. ROBINSON

ABINGDON PRESS
New York · Nashville

PRINTED IN GREAT BRITAIN
BY W. & J. MACKAY & CO LTD, CHATHAM

CONTENTS

PREFACE

THE substance of this book formed the William Belden Noble lectures, given at Harvard University in December 1955. My first word of gratitude must be to the trustees of the lectureship and to all those whose unfailing kindness and generosity to me and my wife made our stay in Cambridge, Mass., such a memorable experience. In particular I must thank Dr Nathan Pusey, President of Harvard University; Dr George Buttrick, Preacher to the Memorial Church within whose walls the lectures were delivered, and Mrs Buttrick, who made themselves responsible for all my arrangements; Dr Douglas Horton and my colleagues at the Harvard Divinity School; and, last but not least, Dr Charles Taylor and my hosts at the Episcopal Theological School.

My gratitude is due also to the Editors of *The Expository Times* and *The Journal of Theological Studies* for permission to reproduce material appearing respectively in chapters II and VII; to those who have been kind enough to read the manuscript and offer their comments: Professor T. W. Manson; Professor K. Stendahl; the Reverend H. W. Montefiore; Mr J. C. O'Neill; and Professor C. F. D. Moule, to whose forbearance and patient criticism almost every idea in this book has been subjected in the course of its development.

The Biblical quotations have been taken from the American Revised Standard Version of the Bible copyrighted 1946 and 1952 by permission of Thomas Nelson & Sons Ltd, Edinburgh, and, in U.S.A., of the Division of Christian Education of the National Council of Churches; at points changes have seemed desirable in order to draw out the sense.

J.A.T.R.

Cambridge, January 1957

INTRODUCTION

'WHENCE he shall come again to judge both the quick and the dead.' For some time the Cinderella of the Credal doctrines, the doctrine of the Second Coming of Christ has now returned to the forefront of theological discussion. But the same modern world which has pressed upon men its relevance has also made problematic its interpretation in any form in which it can be intelligible, and therefore relevant, to the modern mind. And so the insistent question has been that of interpretation: What does it mean for us today? And it is to this question that the growing number of recent books has been addressed.[1] But behind this lies always the prior question, What is it that has to be interpreted? And that is one to which we have tended to assume perhaps too uncritically that we know the answer.

In a pre-critical age, and to the modern Fundamentalist (who still abounds in this field more thickly than in any other), the formulation of the Christian doctrine of the Last Things is a matter of assembling texts and arranging them into a coherent map of the End. Allowance may be made for the poetic or symbolic nature of the language here employed; but fundamentally the Biblical statements are regarded as predictions. And the task of systematic theology, as its name implies, is to co-ordinate these 'prophecies' without contradiction into an ordered sequence of events.

[1]The Second Assembly of the World Council of Churches in 1954, which took the Christian hope for its main theme, stimulated a number of important contributions. They include, apart from its own reports: E. Brunner, *Eternal Hope* (1954); J. E. Fison, *The Christian Hope* (1954); P. S. Minear, *Christian Hope and the Second Coming* (1954); also a bibliography prepared by Minear: *Christ, the Hope of the World.* Cf. the earlier survey compiled by W. Schweitzer, *Eschatology and Ethics* (Study Department of the World Council of Churches, 1951).

9

Against this view, recent writers, while insisting upon the reality of the summing up of all things in Christ, have argued that the true character of the Biblical statements about the end of the world, as about its beginning, is not that of literal history but of myth. The various elements in the New Testament picture of the End are not to be taken as predictions; they represent, rather, theological convictions about the ultimate sovereignty of God in Christ. They are expressed, as they must be if the meaning and reality of the historical process is to be preserved, as vindications of God in history, and therefore as events. But they are not to be viewed as literal occurrences, with a date and place, any more than the 'events' of the Fall. In this way, it is claimed, all the Biblical language can be given its full value, transposed, as it were, into a different key.

But, important and indeed vital as the transposition is for a true understanding of this language and its function, it can, by itself, permit an equally uncritical approach to the doctrine concerned. All the Biblical material may still be used undiscriminatingly for the construction of the Christian picture of the End. The only difference is that it is now a matter of combining images rather than of co-ordinating predictions. And in this it is even easier to be comprehensive without falling into contradiction.[1]

This procedure, as much as that of the Fundamentalists, enables us to evade the critical and historical questions. But, since Christianity is not a system of ideas, but an interpretation of history, no sound or lasting foundation of Christian doctrine can be erected on such evasion. Sooner or later it will be undermined, like a house built on sand.

It is because I believe this process of erosion not to be so distant as we might like to think that I have found myself driven to investigate the foundations. For subterranean rumblings are heard most clearly by those who have their rooms on the ground floor, that is, at the New Testament

[1]A good example of this way of treating the evidence is to be seen in Minear's book cited above.

level of the doctrinal construction. And they are the more noticeable to one who has recently moved downstairs, in the first instance from the floor of the philosophy of religion to that of systematic theology, and then from systematic theology to Biblical studies.

In an earlier book, *In the End, God* . . ., published in 1950, I made a first attempt to bridge the gulf between the New Testament conception of the Last Things and the outlook of the twentieth century. As an essay in interpretation I have no wish to go back upon it, and indeed I must refer the reader to it for such answer as I have to the questions at which this book stops. But it makes the assumption, like most other writing at the doctrinal level, that it is possible to accept the New Testament teaching about the Second Coming more or less as it stands and then to build upon it.

But, when one moves downstairs, one discovers that the New Testament scholars themselves are by no means prepared to do this. One may take, for instance, Professor J. Jeremias' book, *The Parables of Jesus*, one of the outstanding pieces of recent critical scholarship and on the whole conservative in its estimate of our capacity to recover the original teaching of Jesus. There one finds the conclusion that most if not all the familiar parables of waiting for the Lord's return had in the first instance no reference to a Second Coming at all. Or again, in his book *The Christian Hope*, Canon J. E. Fison examines five texts from the Gospels on the Second Coming, which Baron von Hügel selected as being 'of immense weight and luminous clearness, which stand above all suspicion of a secondary origin',[1] and upon which he rested his interpretation of the mind of Jesus. Now Canon Fison has no interest whatever in minimizing these references—in fact his whole book is a protest against any attempt to reduce the idea of the Second Coming out of the Christian Faith. Yet at the end of his cautious examination he has to confess

[1]*Essays and Addresses on the Philosophy of Religion*, p. 123; quoted by Fison, op. cit., p. 187. The texts are Matt. 16.28; 19.28; 24.29 f.; 26.29, 64.

that 'von Hugel's "luminous" texts have been reduced to one'. 'But', he adds, one feels with a certain air of relief, 'the one is enough'.[1]

But this process is, to say the least, disquieting. Even if we have no fears that everything may slip through our fingers, it is clear that it is impossible to reconstruct, let alone interpret, the teaching of Jesus in this matter if the foundations are really as fluid as this. And what Jesus himself taught cannot be irrelevant for the construction of Christian doctrine. It would be impossible simply to be content with the expectation of the New Testament Church, if at this point it could be maintained that it had seriously misconceived the expectation of Jesus. For if the Church represented Jesus as promising to return when he himself gave no such promise, clearly the foundation of the Credal clause and of the whole Christian hope would be imperilled.

I am not saying that this is the situation. But at least there appears to be a case for investigation. No open-minded student of the Gospels would deny that there are signs in the tradition of what scholars call a 'heightening of eschatology'. That is to say, there are sayings of Jesus which in their more original form contain no clear allusion to a second coming, but which later are adapted to speak of it quite specifically. Other sayings, again, have been applied to this event by the Church, when within the setting of the ministry of Jesus himself it appears that they had a different reference. Under the influence of the early Church's own concern, more of the teaching of Jesus tends to become focused more sharply upon this moment. This is a tendency which has long been recognized among New Testament scholars. But its implications, and perhaps its dimensions, do not appear to me to have been taken sufficiently seriously by those whose task it is to sift and formulate the Christian doctrine of the Last Things.

I have therefore felt compelled, in the first instance in order to find a bottom for my own thinking, to dig down to the foundations of this doctrine. How far back does it go? How

[1]Op. cit., p. 194.

did the expectation arise? In what form, if any, does it owe its origin to Jesus? What are the forces that made for its emergence? What is essential to it, what merely peripheral?

It is remarkable how little serious attention has been given to these questions. There are, of course, a great many studies of the eschatology of Jesus,[1] as of the early Church,[2] and some[3] have fastened in particular upon the *delay* or non-occurrence of the Second Coming as an influence in early Christian thinking. But for a systematic inquiry into the origin of the idea itself, and into the relation between Jesus' own expectation and that of the Church, there is only one

[1]Recent contributions include: R. Bultmann, *Jesus* (1926; tr. *Jesus and the Word*, 1935); T. W. Manson, *The Teaching of Jesus* (1931); R. Otto, *Reich Gottes und Menschensohn* (1934; tr. *The Kingdom of God and the Son of Man*, 1938); C. H. Dodd, *The Parables of the Kingdom* (1935); J. Héring, *Le Royaume de Dieu et sa Venue* (1937); A. N. Wilder, *Eschatology and Ethics in the Teaching of Jesus* (1939; 2nd ed. 1950); C. J. Cadoux, *The Historic Mission of Jesus* (1941); W. Manson, *Jesus the Messiah* (1943); W. G. Kümmel, *Verheissung und Erfüllung* (1945; 3rd ed. 1956; tr. *Promise and Fulfilment*, 1957); G. S. Duncan, *Jesus, Son of Man* (1947); J. Jeremias, *Die Gleichnisse Jesu* (2nd ed. 1952; tr. *The Parables of Jesus*, 1954); R. H. Fuller, *The Mission and Achievement of Jesus* (1954); G. R. Beasley-Murray, *Jesus and the Future* (1954). This last contains a full bibliography, as do Wilder and Kümmel. From an earlier date should be mentioned: J. Weiss, *Die Predigt Jesu vom Reiche Gottes* (1892; 2nd ed. 1900); A. Schweitzer, *Das Messianitäts und Leidensgeheimnis: Eine Skizze des Lebens Jesu* (1901; tr. *The Mystery of the Kingdom of God*, 1925); *Von Reimarus zu Wrede* (1906; tr. *The Quest of the Historical Jesus*, 1910); E. von Dobschütz, *The Eschatology of the Gospels* (1910).

[2]E.g., H. A. A. Kennedy, *St Paul's Conceptions of the Last Things* (1904); C. H. Dodd, *The Apostolic Preaching and its Developments* (1936); H. A. Guy, *The New Testament Doctrine of the Last Things* (1948); C. K. Barrett, 'New Testament Eschatology', *Scottish Journal of Theology*, VI (1953), pp. 136–55; 225–43; B. Rigaux, *Les Épitres aux Thessaloniciens* (1956), and the exhaustive bibliography there provided.

[3]E.g., M. Werner, *Die Entstehung des christlichen Dogmas* (1941); H. Conzelmann, *Die Mitte der Zeit* (1954), and the bibliography there given.

book known to me, Dr T. F. Glasson's study, *The Second Advent: The Origin of the New Testament Doctrine,* published in 1945. Partly because of war conditions, but more largely, I suspect, because its conclusions cut across much contemporary thinking, or lack of it, in the Church, this book has not received the recognition which it would seem to me to deserve. It is a good deal easier to sneer at its presuppositions[1] than to meet its arguments. I should like to record my indebtedness to it, which is much greater than the occasional footnote would suggest. At many points my difficulty has been to avoid duplicating its arguments, and where in what follows the ground has been covered lightly, it is usually because it seemed more useful to pursue questions which Dr Glasson did not ask than to go over again those which to my satisfaction he has answered.

One merit of Dr Glasson's book, as of Dr C. H. Dodd's *Parables of the Kingdom,* is its capacity to speak to the general reader at the same time as it provides the scholar with the evidence he needs for checking its judgements. I have also tried, though under no illusion of success, to write at these two levels at once. In a piece of New Testament study, especially one whose conclusions will often challenge accepted assumptions, the student has the right to the detailed exegesis and argument on which it is based and the necessary references to the sources and authorities. But these have been kept to a minimum, and, where possible, like all allusion to the Greek text, been reserved for footnotes.

Nothing lasting will be achieved at the expense of scholarship. But this book is written with more than a purely academic interest. For, if I am right in the analysis of my earlier book, the Church finds itself today in much the same position in regard to its doctrine of the Last Things as our grandfathers did a century ago in relation to the First Things. It is here that obscurantism, whether in regard to Biblical criticism or to the perspectives of contemporary science, can

[1]As is done, for instance, by G. R. Beasley-Murray, op. cit., pp. 30 f.

most easily provide the occasion for rejecting the whole Christian scheme of thought. The passions and follies on both sides have been mitigated in the course of a hundred years. But there is little sign that, from the Christian side, the reappraisal is likely this time to be much more acceptable. When it is remembered how much agony was necessary previously in order to sift the wheat from the chaff, we shall not underestimate what is involved when it is not simply the words of Moses which are at stake but those of Christ himself.

Furthermore, though much of this investigation will be critical in nature, its ultimate concern is with construction, not with criticism. It may look, as the argument advances, as if its conclusions promise to be negative. That is certainly not the intention, nor, I trust, the outcome. My purpose could not be expressed better than by the Author of the Epistle to the Hebrews who, when himself writing of Christian eschatology, speaks in 12.27 of 'the removal of what is shaken . . . in order that what cannot be shaken may remain'. And he continues: 'Let us therefore give thanks for having received a kingdom that cannot be shaken, and let us offer to God acceptable worship, with reverence and awe'. The conclusion is not irrelevant. For it is precisely, as I shall hint at the close, in the worship of the Church that the split that we shall detect between the first and second comings is resolved, the Last Supper and the Great Supper converge, and the Christ who came and the Christ who shall come are known in the Christ who comes.

THE CHURCH'S EXPECTATION OF CHRIST

THE subject of our investigation is the expectation of Christ. And the very phrase contains within it the two aspects of the matter whose inter-connexion will be our chief concern. These can be expressed the one by a statement and the other by a question. The Church expected Jesus: What did Jesus expect? The problem before us is the relation between the two. Is the answer to the question to be found in the statement, or not? Did the Church, that is to say, expect Jesus because Jesus himself expected to return, and so led his Church to await him?

In this first chapter we shall consider the statement. We shall examine the actual expectation of the early Church regarding the return of her Lord. In the second and third we shall go to the evidence of the Gospels, to trace as far as we may the expectation of Jesus himself. In the next three an attempt will be made to see how the one expectation is related to the other, historically and theologically. Finally, in the last chapter, we shall ask ourselves, in the light of all this, what conclusion emerges from the New Testament, for its hope and for ours.

First, then, the statement: the Church expected Jesus. That at least is not open to dispute. It is as widely attested throughout the New Testament as any article of the Christian Creed—in the four Gospels, the Acts, the Epistles, the Apocalypse. Among the twenty-seven books, the Advent hope is absent only from Galatians, Ephesians, Philemon and II and III

16

John; and in each of these, with the exception probably of Ephesians, the fact that it does not occur is almost certainly fortuitous. This is not to say that it is uniformly prominent. Indeed, in some writings, notably the fourth Gospel, it is, in its traditional form, virtually absent, and that there was at least a shift of emphasis on this matter in the mind of Paul is, I believe, undeniable. But these variations belong to the history and development of the idea. At the moment we are concerned simply with the evidence for its existence, and for this a single instance is sufficient.

But, to make progress, it is necessary to probe and analyse further the contents of this expectation. For the *coming* of Christ is but one element in a whole complex of ideas which together made up the hope of the early Church. These ideas merged with each other in an ill-defined manner and the separate strands are not readily isolated.

Indeed, the very name of what we are seeking to describe is not fixed within the New Testament. The 'Second Coming' or 'Second Advent' is not itself a Biblical expression, and it first occurs as late as the middle of the second century A.D. The word in the New Testament nearest to becoming a technical term is *parousia* (the Greek for 'presence' or 'coming'), which, for convenience, is that which we shall normally use, since it has become the recognized term in theological discussion. But even this occurs, of the coming of Christ, in only four passages in the New Testament (I Cor. 15.23; James 5.7 f.; II Peter 3.4 and I John 2.28) outside the Thessalonian epistles and a single chapter of Matthew (24). Moreover, it is not, apparently, until the third century, with Clement of Alexandria, that we find 'the *Parousia*' used technically by itself without some qualifying genitive like 'of Jesus Christ'—and then for Clement it means not the Second Coming but the Incarnation![1]

By far the commonest way of expressing this hope was simply to employ the verb 'to come', though the noun from

[1]For the evidence *vide* A. Oepke in G. Kittel, *Theologisches Wörterbuch zum N.T.*, V, 856–69.

this root, *eleusis*, is never so used, despite the fact that it was employed by the Jews of the coming of the Messiah, while *parousia* was not.[1] Other terms are the revelation,[2] the appearing,[3] and the day,[4] of Christ; while it is also said of him that he will be manifested,[5] seen,[6] and revealed.[7]

Provisionally, we may describe the distinctive element that concerns us by defining it as *the expectation of the coming of Christ from heaven to earth in manifest and final glory.* It is this we shall refer to by the term *Parousia*, and it forms the distinctively Christian centre of the New Testament hope. Associated with it, however, are other elements in the traditional eschatology, or picture of the End, which in origin are distinct but which in Christianity have been merged in it. Four of these may be isolated for discussion: (1) The day of the Lord; (2) The last judgement; (3) The ingathering of the elect; and (4) The end of the world.

(1) The first of these traditional elements we have already encountered in the phrase 'the day of Christ'. This expression is closely associated in the New Testament with the *Parousia*. Thus, Paul combines the two ideas in I Cor. 1.7 f.:

[1]Cf. G. D. Kilpatrick, 'Acts 7.52, ἔλευσις,', *Journal of Theological Studies,* XLVI (1945), pp. 136–45. It is interesting that whereas Paul uses the noun παρουσία and the verb πάρειμι indifferently of himself, the latter is never in the New Testament used of the expected coming of Christ, despite the fact that it occurs of the coming of 'the one like a son of man' in the Septuagint of Dan. 7.13. The noun is regularly παρουσία and the verb ἔρχομαι.

[2]ἀποκάλυψις: I Cor. 1.7; II Thess. 1.7; I Peter 1.7 and 13; 4.13 (cf. II Baruch 29.3; IV Ezra 7.28; 13.32).

[3]ἐπιφάνεια: II Thess. 2.8; I Tim. 6.14; II Tim. 4.1, 8; Tit. 2.13.

[4]Specifically of Christ, or the Lord (= Jesus), or the Son of man: Matt. 24.42; Luke 17.22–31; I Cor. 1.8; 5.5; II Cor. 1.14; Phil. 1.6, 10; 2.16; I Thess. 5.2–4; II Thess. 2.2 (cf. IV Ezra 13.52).

[5]φανεροῦμαι: Col. 3.4; I Peter 5.4; I John 2.28; 3.2. φανέρωσις, perhaps surprisingly, is never so used. ἐμφανίζω occurs in John 14.21 f.

[6]ὁρῶμαι: Heb. 9.28. Cf. Mark 13.26 and parallels; 14.62 and par.; John 1.51; 16.16–19; I John 3.2; Rev.1.7; and the similar use of θεωρέω in John 6.62; 14.19.

[7]ἀποκαλύπτομαι: Luke 17.30.

'As you wait for the *revealing* of our Lord Jesus Christ; (God) will sustain you to the end, guiltless in the *day* of our Lord Jesus Christ.'

Again, in the Thessalonian letters (I Thess. 4.15–5.11; II Thess. 2.1 f.), as in II Peter (3.1–10), 'the coming of the Lord' and 'the day of the Lord' are equated. Yet it is clear that 'the day of the Lord Jesus' is in itself simply the traditional 'day of the Lord' of the Old Testament, with Christ, 'the Lord' of the Christian community, taking the place of Yahweh. Indeed, there are passages in the New Testament (e.g. Acts 2.20) where the phrase 'the day of the Lord' still means what it is actually called as late as II Peter 3.12, 'the day of *God*'. And this 'day' had no necessary association with a 'coming' of God to his people, let alone with a coming of his Christ. Indeed, the 'coming one' of Malachi 3 and 4 is explicitly promised '*before* the great and terrible day of the Lord' (4.5). In itself, 'the day of the Lord' is a general and comprehensive expression for the consummation of God's purpose, alike in victory and in judgement. And in the New Testament, as in the Old, 'the day' (I Cor. 3.13; Heb. 10.25) or 'that day' (II Tim. 1.12, 18; 4.8) is simply an abbreviation for the day of judgement (Matt. 10.15, etc.; II Peter 2.9; I John 4.17), of wrath (Rom. 2.5), or visitation (I Peter 2.12), which is, from the other side, the day of redemption (Eph. 4.30).

Now all this is taken over in Christianity and interpreted as the consummation of all things in Christ; and there are passages, as when Paul prays that the Philippians may be 'pure and blameless for the day of Christ' (Phil. 1.10; cf. 1.6 and 2.16), where one would not need to suppose anything more to be implied than the traditional day of judgement, viewed now as a judgement dispensed by Christ.[1] In fact it is also associated by Paul with a *coming* of Christ in glory from heaven, but 'the day' would not of itself imply or suggest this. Moreover, for the *origin* of the phrase there is no need to

[1]Cf. the alternation between 'the judgement seat of God' (Rom. 14.10) and 'the judgement seat of Christ' (II Cor. 5.10).

look beyond the Old Testament, modified now by the definition of God in the face of Jesus Christ.

(2) Secondly, and, as we have seen, intimately associated with 'the day', is the element of judgement. This again is closely connected with the *Parousia* expectation; so much so that most commentators have only to read in Acts 10.42 that Jesus is 'ordained by God to be judge of the living and the dead' to assume that Peter proclaimed he was to '*come again* to judge the quick and the dead'. But the fact that the judgement is to be exercised by or through Christ does not in itself imply a *Parousia*,[1] though this is, of course, frequently associated with it.[2] All it indicates is that the traditional idea of the judgement of the world by *God*, which is still in fact the commoner form of expression in the New Testament,[3] is being given a specifically Christian content. When the *Parousia* becomes the central feature of the End, then naturally the ideas of judgement and retribution cluster around it; but they are part of the conception of the End, whether a return in glory is envisaged or not.

(3) A third element in the traditional expectation, which in the New Testament is associated with the *Parousia*, is that of the ingathering of the elect. This combination occurs only in the apocalyptic discourses of Mark (13.26 f.) and Matt. (24.30 f.) and in the Pauline Epistles, where the idea of a corporate *parousia*, of Christ and his saints reunited to him, is a notable feature.[4] But, again, the reassembly of the scattered People of God is already a regular element in the eschatological hope of Judaism (e.g. Isa. 11.12; Jer. 31.8), and does not of

[1]There is no suggestion of it, for instance, in such passages as: Matt. 10.32 f. = Luke 12.8 f.; John 3.18 f.; 5.22–30; Acts 17.31; Rom. 2.16; II Cor. 5.10.

[2]Mark 8.38 and pars; Matt. 25.31 ff.; I Cor. 4.4 f.; II Thess. 1.7–10; 2.8; II Tim. 4.1; James 5.7–9; cf. and contrast John 16.8.

[3]e.g. Rom. 2.2–5; 14.10–12; Heb. 10.30 f.; 12.23; 13.4; I Peter 2.23; Rev. 6.10; 14.7; 18.8.

[4]I Thess. 4.17; II Thess. 1.10; 2.1; Col. 3.4; cf. Phil. 3.20 f. In I Thess. 3.13 the 'holy ones' may be angels, as in Zech. 14.5; but cf. *The Didache* xvi,7 for taking it as 'saints'.

itself imply or require a coming of the Christ in glory from heaven.

(4) Finally, the *Parousia* is naturally associated with 'the end of all things' (I Peter 4.7), 'the last hour' (I John 2.18; cf. I Peter 1.5); and the imminence of the *Parousia* is the imminence of the end of the world.[1] Now, the supersession of this world order is again an integral part of 'the day of the Lord' (cf. II Peter 3.10–13), and when this latter is identified with the day of Christ it is natural that Christians should speak in a single breath of his 'coming and the close of the age' (Matt. 24.3). But, once more, the end of the world does not in itself presuppose a *parousia*, and, of course, forms part of traditional expectations that know nothing of it. Moreover, it is noteworthy that while the fourth Gospel retains the concept of 'the last day' (John 6.39–54; 11.24; 12.48) its doctrine of the *Parousia* is entirely dissociated from it. The judgement of the world for this Gospel, like the resurrection of the dead, belongs indeed to 'the last day', though it is not confined to it; but the coming of Christ is nowhere related to it.

The point of these somewhat artificial distinctions between different elements in the tradition is twofold. First, these ideas, and others like them,[2] which in the New Testament are associated with the *Parousia*, do not of themselves require any special explanation. The consummation of God's purpose, the judgement, the ingathering, and the end of the world are all part of traditional Jewish eschatology. And they could have been brought into line with the revelation that 'the end of the Lord' (James 5.11) was none other than Jesus Christ without involving the expectation that 'this Jesus, who was

---

[1]Thus, in Mark 13 and pars. 'the End' is evidently intended to be equated with the moment of 'the *Parousia*'. In I Cor. 15.23 f. they are probably to be distinguished.

[2]E.g. the resurrection of the dead. Usually in the New Testament this is not brought into explicit relation with the *Parousia*, but the connexion is made, in the case of the Christian dead, in I Thess. 4.14–17 and I Cor. 15.23, 52.

taken up from you into heaven, will come in the same way as
you saw him go' (Acts 1.11). It is this particular element in
the Christian hope whose origin we are seeking. And this
element is precisely the one that is not part of the traditional
Jewish scheme. The Jews did not speak of the *parousia* of
the Messiah, they did not expect that he would descend with
clouds from heaven,[1] and above all they did not expect that
he would come back once he had come.[2] If this is the peculiar
feature it is important to isolate it, if only for examination,
from other features in the New Testament hope which are
not.

[1]This, I believe, has been demonstrated conclusively by Glasson,
op. cit., pp. 13–62; cf. p. 168: 'Nowhere in the whole range of O.T.
prophecy, pre-Christian apocalyptic and Gospel teaching, is the
word "descend" used of the Messiah'. Apart from a vague reference
in Orac. Sib. 5.414 f. (second century A.D.?), the first appearance of
this idea in Judaism seems to be in Joshua ben Levi (c. 250 A.D.),
who combines Dan. 7.13 with Zech. 9.9: 'If they (Israel) are worthy,
he comes with the clouds of heaven; if they are not worthy, then
lowly and riding on an ass' (Strack-Billerbeck, *Kommentar zum
N.T.*, I, p. 843). For further evidence from post-Christian Judaism,
vide Glasson, op. cit., pp. 218–31.

[2]The only possible reference to this is in II Baruch 30.1 (c. 90 A.D.):
'When the time of the advent of the Messiah is fulfilled, and he will
return in glory, then all who have fallen asleep in him shall rise
again'. This is almost certainly a Christian interpolation (Oepke
and Glasson). But if original it must refer to the return of the
Messiah *to heaven*. (R. H. Charles, *Apocrypha and Pseudepigrapha
of the O.T.*, ad. loc.)

A. Dupont Sommer has recently revived the view of S. Schechter
(*Documents of Jewish Sectaries,* I, pp. xii ff.) that the Zadokite Frag-
ment (CDC) and now the Habakkuk Commentary from the Dead Sea
Scrolls (1QpH) speak of the Teacher of Righteousness appearing
first as the Community's founder, when he suffered death at the
hand of his enemies, and then at 'the end of the days' coming
again as the Messiah (*The Dead Sea Scrolls*, pp. 25–44, 99). This, it
is to be noted, certainly does not imply *two* comings of *the Christ*
and would be in line rather with the conception to be found in the
speech of Acts 3 (*vide* below ch. VII). But this interpretation is in
any case based upon a very doubtful reading of the evidence. Cf.
F. M. Cross, 'The Essenes and their Master', *The Christian Century,*

And the second point of the abstraction is this. It is often said that for the early Church the Second Coming *was* the Christian hope. Remove this and one would be left with a completely realized eschatology, a hope, that is to say, exhausted in the first coming of Christ, with no element of futurity left save that of sheer finality.

Now no one would wish to deny that the *Parousia* was the expectation in which all the elements in the Biblical hope found new focus and unity. But these other elements would still have been there even had they not come to be associated with the expectation of the Christ's return. For clearly they had not yet been fulfilled. Even after the Resurrection it was obvious to all, except to a few fanatics at Thessalonica (II Thess. 2.2), that 'the day of the Lord' had not come in any final sense; and it was equally evident that the ingathering of the elect, the general resurrection, the last judgement, and the end of this present world-order had all still to take place. It was inconceivable that any Jew could abandon these expectations. And there is equally no reason to doubt that, baptized into Christ, they formed the framework of every Christian's view of the future, whether or not he linked them with the fresh element in his hope, the personal return of Jesus Christ.

That all things were to be consummated in Christ was a hope that no Christian could forgo without jettisoning his faith altogether: to deny it would be to deny the sovereignty of God in Christ over the future as over the past and present. Yet it is noteworthy that nowhere does this conviction, of the summing up of all things in Christ, come to more resounding expression than in the Epistle to the Ephesians—the one major document in which the *Parousia* receives no

LXXII, 33 (Aug. 17, 1955), pp. 944 f.; M. Black, 'Theological Conceptions in the Dead Sea Scrolls', *Svensk Exegetisk Årsbok*, XVIII–XIX (1953–4), pp. 85 f.; M. Burrows, *The Dead Sea Scrolls*, pp. 265 f.

Though Judaism entertained the idea of a Moses or Elijah *redivivus*, the notion of a Christ *redivivus* would have seemed an absurdity.

mention.[1] This is not to say that its writer did not share this expectation. But it shows how the essence of the Christian hope could still find expression without any reference to it. It is not the case that without this particular expectation the whole Christian hope for the future and of God's final control over it must fall to the ground.

So far we have simply sought to isolate for inspection that element in the Christian hope which is our particular concern, the expectation, namely, of the coming of Christ from heaven to earth in manifest and final glory. We have now to ask the question: 'Where did this expectation come from?'—absent as it is from Judaism and the Old Testament, universal as it is, with minor exceptions, in the documents of the New Testament.

There is one explanation which would settle the issue at once, namely, that it came from him who himself stood between the Testaments. The early Christians, that is to say, expected Jesus because Jesus himself taught them to expect him. This is on all counts the most obvious explanation, and the burden of proof lies squarely on anyone who would deny it. It is then to Jesus' own words, and therefore to the evidence of the Gospels, that we are driven. And this evidence will occupy us in the next two chapters. But first, let us see what further light may be derived from the other documents of the New Testament, those, that is, which reflect directly the Church's own understanding of its message. How did *it* see the origin of its hope?

Now it is noteworthy that the Epistles nowhere attempt to account for the belief which everywhere they presuppose. They do not tell us where it came from; and they never claim that it goes back to Jesus. II Peter 3.4 speaks of 'the promise of his coming', but it is not stated that the promise was made by Jesus. Indeed, the subsequent words, 'the Lord is not slow about his promise' (v. 9) must almost certainly in the

[1]Galatians is not concerned with the End at all, so its absence there is hardly significant.

context refer to God. In I Thess. 4.15 Paul appeals to 'a word of the Lord' in connexion with the relative position of the living and dead at the moment of the *Parousia*. But as no one has been able to decide which words in the context, if any, could be words of Jesus,[1] the passage is not very helpful.

It is rather surprising too to discover that the book of Acts does not base the *Parousia* hope on a promise of Jesus. It goes out of its way to make the connexion in the case of the Holy Spirit (Acts 1.4 f.; 2.33; cf. Luke 24.49), even ascribing to Jesus himself (Acts 1.5; 11.16) the promise of baptism not with water but with the Spirit which Luke's own Gospel, like the others, attributes to John the Baptist (Luke 3.16 and pars.). But, in the very same passage (Acts 1.10 f.), the guarantee of Jesus' return is grounded in no word of the Lord but simply in the assurance of the two men in white, who on

---

[1]The two most probable explanations seem to me either (*a*) that the words relate to vv. 16 f. in which Paul cites an early Christian apocalypse as a 'word of the Lord', i.e. a 'prophecy' of the living Christ speaking to and through his Church (So M. Dibelius in Lietzmann's *Handbuch zum N.T.*, ad loc. J. Jeremias, *Unbekannte Jesusworte*[2], pp. 62–4, regards these two verses as a genuine *agraphon*, which appears to me improbable in the extreme; cf. B. Rigaux, op. cit., ad loc.); or (*b*) that the phrase refers back to the assurance in v. 14 that, as Jesus died and rose, so God, through Jesus, will bring with him those who have fallen asleep—not, that is to say, from heaven to earth, but from the grave to share his risen life. We may compare II Cor. 4.14: 'Knowing that he who raised the Lord Jesus will raise us also with Jesus and bring us with you into his presence'. This 'knowledge' or, in Thessalonians, 'faith' is grounded on a word of Jesus himself ('We say this to you ἐν λόγῳ κυρίου'). Paul does not claim actually to be quoting the *logion*, and so it is impossible to identify it. At least, however, we have in John 14.3, 'And when I go and prepare a place for you, I will come again and will take you to myself, that where I am you may be also', a word of Jesus that fits the meaning, which is more than can be said of other interpretations. This second alternative does not appear to have had the consideration it deserves. If true, it would support the suspicion that we have in the eschatological discourse of the Fourth Gospel (John 14–16) traditional material at least as authentic as in its Synoptic counterparts (cf. pp. 172–6 below).

this occasion do not even recall a saying of Jesus, as they do at the empty tomb (Luke 24.4–7). This difference merits, I believe, more reflection than perhaps it has received.

However, the silence of the documents on the origin of the hope must not be pressed, for they were not written to provide an answer to this question. It is more important to see how far back the belief can in fact be traced within the documents themselves.

The first mention of the *Parousia* hope is in I Thess. 1.10. It goes back, that is to say, to what is very likely our earliest Epistle. And indeed it goes back behind it. For Paul is here speaking of his original visit to Thessalonica. He has no need, he writes, to speak of the faith of the Thessalonians, for the Christians of Macedonia and Achaia 'report what a welcome (or, entry) we had among you, and how you turned to God from idols to serve a living and true God, and to wait for his Son from heaven'. Paul does not actually say that he preached the *Parousia* at Thessalonica, but the inference is clear; and indeed it is implied in the whole of the Thessalonian correspondence. This then takes us back to about the year A.D. 50. Can we get any further?

In I Cor. 16.22 we have the Aramaic watchword *marana tha*, 'Come, our Lord!' Now this obviously has its roots in early Palestinian Christianity and by the time Paul wrote to the predominantly Gentile church of Corinth had already established itself as a liturgical formula beyond need of translation.[1] This would be extremely important evidence, could we be sure what it means. But in the first place it is impossible to be certain whether it should be taken as an imperative, 'Our Lord, come!', or as an indicative, 'Our Lord is come!'. On the assumption that the prayer in Rev. 22.20, 'Come, Lord Jesus', represents a Greek version of it, the imperative is probably the more natural, though a good case can be argued either way.[2] But even if it is a prayer to Jesus

---

[1] It recurs in a similar liturgical context in *The Didache* x, 6, along with two other untranslated words (ὡσαννά and ἀμήν).

[2] *Vide* K. G. Kuhn in Kittel, *T.W.N.T.*, IV, pp. 470 ff.

to come to his own, the fact that it almost certainly has its context in the primitive Eucharist[1] raises the question whether it means more than what is implied, say, in Rev. 3.20: 'Behold, I stand at the door and knock; if any one hears my voice and opens the door, I will *come in* to him and eat with him, and he with me.' Of course, it is possible that the coming of Christ to his own in the liturgy is viewed simply as an anticipation of his coming at the *Parousia*. But that is to beg the question. The single phrase *marana tha* cannot by itself tell us anything certain. And even if we could be sure how Paul interpreted it, its pre-Pauline significance is obscure.

But can we get behind Paul at any other point? The next difficulty that meets us is that though he makes it clear that *he* preached the *Parousia* hope, nowhere does he refer to it as part of the tradition that he himself 'received'. Its spread throughout the New Testament is against any suggestion that it was a peculiarly Pauline doctrine, for which there is no evidence whatever. But, for the purposes of tracking the concept back, his silence at this point about the common tradition is disappointing. Nor are we any better off when we move outside the Pauline Epistles. None of the other Epistles afford any hints, and the *Parousia* is not mentioned among the 'foundation' beliefs listed by the Epistle to the Hebrews in 6.1 f., though eschatology is well represented in 'the resurrection of the dead' and 'eternal judgment'.

We are left then with the speeches at the beginning of Acts for evidence of the early preaching. Naturally, if these are purely Lucan constructions put into the mouth of Peter and Paul, they provide no primitive evidence at all. But I am convinced that the theology and vocabulary of the earlier speeches do afford confidence that there is here genuinely primitive material, from which it is possible to reconstruct a reasonably trustworthy picture of the earliest Apostolic preaching.[2]

---

[1] *Vide* my note, 'Traces of a Liturgical Sequence in I. Cor. 16.20–24', in *The Journal of Theological Studies* (N.S.), IV (1953), pp. 38–41.

[2] *Vide* C. H. Dodd, *The Apostolic Preaching and its Developments*, pp. 17–20, and ch. VII below.

Now, it is generally assumed that these speeches contain a doctrine of the *Parousia*. But there are in fact only two possible references, and neither, I believe, is convincing.

One is in Acts 10.42, which has already been mentioned. Here the Apostles are commanded to testify that Jesus is the one '*ordained* by God as judge of the living and the dead'. The Greek verb is the same as that used in Rom. 1.4, where Jesus is spoken of as '*designated* Son of God in power . . . by his resurrection from the dead', and in Acts 17.31, where it is said that God 'will judge the world . . . by a man whom he has *appointed*, and of this he has given assurance . . . by raising him from the dead'. In these, as in other similar passages, Jesus is conceived as given his titles of glory by virtue of the Resurrection.[1] That he is judge *is* what the Apostles are commissioned to preach. His function as judge is clearly not yet exhausted, but there is no suggestion that he will be judge only at some second coming, no mention of which in fact is made.

The other passage occurs in the speech of Acts 3, where the Jews are urged to repent that 'times of refreshing may come from the presence of the Lord, and that he may send the Christ appointed for you, even Jesus, whom heaven must receive until the time of the restoration of all things' (Acts 3.20 f.). This passage I mention, only to reserve for full discussion at a subsequent stage. It will in fact receive extended treatment in chapter VII, as I believe it to be of great importance for our theme. But I hope to show that its reference is not in fact to a return or *second* coming of Christ; for, according to the theology of this speech, Jesus has not yet come *as the Christ* at all. The passage is of crucial significance for the origin of the *Parousia* doctrine; but I do not think that it actually embodies that belief—and it is for the existence of the belief at the earliest stage that we are at present looking.

If this is so, we are left with the surprising conclusion that

[1]Cf. Acts 2.32–6 (Lord and Christ); 5.31 (Leader and Saviour); 13.33 (Son).

no evidence is to be found that the *Parousia* expectation formed part of the earliest strata of Apostolic Christianity.

There is, naturally, a great gulf between establishing the silence of the evidence and the absence of the belief. The fact that all the paths by which one might hope to trace the belief back into the common *kerygma*, or preaching, of the primitive Church get lost in the sand is not lightly to be dismissed. But it cannot be regarded as decisive. For the argument from silence is, as always, precarious. To take but one instance, we should not gather from Acts that Paul preached this doctrine, whereas we known for certain that he did.

There are, however, two factors which may suggest that this silence is not entirely fortuitous.

In the first place, the gospel message as presented in the Acts summaries does not read as if it has had its last term lopped off or accidentally omitted. On the contrary, it has a clear climax of its own which requires no addition. An example of this climax is to be found in the close of Peter's Pentecost sermon in Acts 2.32–6:

'This Jesus God raised up, and of that we all are witnesses. Being therefore exalted at the right hand of God, and having received from the Father the promise of the Holy Spirit, he has poured out this which you see and hear. For David did not ascend into the heavens; but he himself says,

"The Lord said to my Lord, Sit at my right hand, till I make thy enemies a stool for thy feet."

Let all the house of Israel therefore know assuredly that God has made him both Lord and Christ, this Jesus whom you crucified.'

The position represented by this speech is as follows. The final outpouring of the Spirit has now taken place (2.17), the messianic age has been inaugurated, and Christ henceforth must rule till all his foes submit. The end of this reign will coincide (presumably) with the day of the Lord, the great and manifest day (2.20), when, with the full tale of the elect (2.39), God's purpose will be complete.

We have here what might be called a fully *inaugurated*

eschatology. All is not yet summed up; yet all that is to be has now been set in motion. There remains, strongly, an element of 'until'; yet it is of a *reign* until. The Christ is not expected so much as *expecting*, waiting, till his finished work runs its course. The decisive messianic act itself is complete: there is not a part of it still to come. The picture of the regnant and expectant Lord can therefore stand as the climax of the Acts speeches without producing any sense of inconclusiveness.

The same is true of the kerygmatic hymn of Phil. 2.6–11. This has an exactly similar climax in the exaltation of Jesus as the Lord of glory, to the final end that 'at the name of Jesus every knee should bow, in heaven and on earth and under the earth'. This is, of course, in no way *incompatible* with the expectation that this Jesus shall later come again *from* heaven. Indeed, Paul explicitly combines the two ideas later in the same Epistle: 'Our commonwealth is in heaven, and *from it we await a saviour,* the Lord Jesus Christ, who will change our lowly body, by the power which enables him *even to subject all things to himself'* (Phil. 3.20 f.). But no one could say that the hymn demands the *Parousia* as its climax, or that it is obviously lacking an element needed to complete it.

A corollary of this is perhaps to be seen in the confusion which results when Paul does introduce the element of the *Parousia* into the kind of pattern we have just described. In I Cor. 15.24–8 we have the same conception of the End in terms of the ultimate reduction of all things to the rule of Christ (followed, uniquely here, by the subjection of Christ himself to God):

'Then comes the end, when he delivers the kingdom to God the Father after destroying every rule and every authority and power. For he must reign until he has put all his enemies under his feet. The last enemy to be destroyed is death. "For God has put all things in subjection under his feet." But when it says, "All things are put in subjection under him," it is plain that he is excepted who put all things under him. When all things are subjected to him, then the Son himself will also be subjected to him who put all things under him, that God may be everything to every one.'

This reads like a self-contained and very primitive attempt to relate the new fact of the sovereign reign of Christ to the traditional conviction of the final supremacy of God. The scheme is, however, complicated by Paul's previous introduction, in vv. 22 f., of the idea of the *Parousia*:

'For as in Adam all die, so also in Christ shall all be made alive. But each in his own order: Christ the first fruits, then at his coming those who belong to Christ.'

The Apostle seems here to envisage a three-stage eschatology: (i) the Resurrection of Christ, (ii) the *Parousia* (accompanied by the resurrection of Christians), and (iii) the End (accompanied by the general resurrection). This last marks the end of the reign of Christ and the handing back of the kingdom to the Father.

The difficulty is to know where in this scheme the reign of Christ *begins*. Probably Paul means that it has already begun with the first moment (that of the Resurrection)—'for God *has* put all things in subjection under his feet'—and that it will go on till the third—'for he must reign until he has put all his enemies under his feet'. This is the eschatology of the primitive preaching. It is not easy, however, to see then precisely what is the significance of the second moment, that of the *Parousia*.

One interpretation is to treat the second and third moments as virtually simultaneous: the *Parousia* represents the end of Christ's reign in the reduction of the last enemy, *and this means* the End itself has come, when the sovereignty given to the Son is returned to the Father. This, however, is not the natural way to take the sequence 'then at his coming . . . then comes the end', a form of expression[1] which earlier in the chapter—'then he appeared to James, then to all the apostles' (15.7)—clearly indicates two *separate* stages in a temporal series. And this is borne out by the fact that the dead in Christ rise *first*, presumably to a share in the kingdom,

[1] ἔπειτα . . . εἶτα.

not of God, but of Christ, in which the mass of mankind do not participate.

Others, consequently, have taken the *Parousia* to mark the *beginning* of the reign of Christ, and have found here the roots of that chiliastic development in Christian theology represented in the millennium of Rev. 20.4–6. On this reading, the *Parousia*, instead of being equated with the final day of the Lord, is viewed as preceding it by a considerable interval. Expectations in late Jewish apocalyptic of a limited reign of the Messiah prior to the End (cf. IV Ezra 7.28 f.; II Baruch 30.1; 40.3) are cited in support, but applied to the second coming of the Christ, not his first. But there are grave difficulties also in the way of this interpretation. The past tense, 'God has put all things in subjection under him', indicating that the messianic rule has already begun, and the identification elsewhere in Paul of the *Parousia* (or 'day of Christ') with 'the day of the Lord', are against it.

It will be observed, however, how in each case the difficulties derive from Paul's introduction of a second messianic moment into the primitive scheme, which viewed the End as a direct consummation of the sovereignty of Christ established at the Resurrection. The *Parousia*, so far from being required by this scheme, is by no means easy to fit into it.

There is, moreover, a second factor which suggests that we are here in the presence of a theology from which the mention of a *Parousia* has not been accidentally or fortuitously omitted. This is the evidence, parallel to that of the primitive preaching summaries, of the earliest credal statements.

In his short but extremely important study, *The Earliest Christian Confessions,* Professor Oscar Cullmann has analysed the formulae latent in the New Testament that provide the first evidence of what the Apostolic Church itself regarded as the irreducible 'essence of Christianity'. He concludes his investigation with the words: 'It is, then, the *present* Lordship of Christ, inaugurated by his resurrection and exaltation to the right hand of God, that is the centre of the faith of primitive Christianity' (p. 58). This conviction is expressed most

succinctly in the briefest of all the formulae: *Kyrios Iesous*,
'Jesus is Lord' (Rom. 10.9; I Cor. 12.3; cf. Phil. 2.11; Col.
2.6). It is reflected more fully in what may be the earliest of the
expanded confessions we possess, representing perhaps the
baptismal creed at Rome at a time before any of our Gospels
were written. This is the passage in I Peter 3.18–22, which,
with the homiletic insertion on the meaning of baptism omitted,
affirms of Christ that he was

'put to death in the flesh
but made alive in the spirit; . . .
who has gone into heaven
and is at the right hand of God,
with angels, authorities, and powers subject to him.'

The similarity of this climax with that of the speeches in Acts
will at once be apparent.

What Cullmann sums up as 'the *present* Lordship of Christ,
inaugurated by his resurrection and exaltation to the right
hand of God' is not intended in any way to deny that the
early Church saw Christ as Lord of the future also. What does
seem to be clear, however, is that it is not until the second
century that this hope is felt to require for its basis a separate
affirmation that he will come in glory and judgement.[1] Before
that there is no clause in any *confessional* statement corresponding to the 'whence he shall come again' of the Apostles'
Creed.[2] This is indeed a remarkable fact, when we recall the

[1]Cullmann detects its first occurrence in a confessional formula
towards the end of the first century, in II Tim. 4.1: 'I charge you in
the presence of God and of Christ Jesus who is to judge the living
and the dead, and by his appearing and his kingdom.' There is,
however, little to suggest that this can properly by called a credal
formula at all. It is in a different class from I Tim. 3.16, where the
climax, as before, is the Ascension.

[2]There is only, it would appear, one instance in the Apostolic
Fathers, namely, in Polycarp, *Phil.* ii, 1. It is absent from the
formulae in Ignatius, and from all but two of the many in Justin
(*Dial.* cxxvi, 1; cxxxii, 1). For the evidence *vide* J. N. D. Kelly,
Early Christian Creeds, ch. III.

numerous references to the *Parousia* throughout the New Testament writings. However vivid its expectation of Jesus, the Church remained content to express its certainty about the future as part of its conviction of the present and continuing sovereignty of Christ, already enthroned as history's Lord and history's Judge. Its eschatology is not a separate department, grounded in a different and still future event: it is subsumed under its Christology, part of what is meant by the fact that God has made Jesus *from now on* both Lord and Christ. Even while it most ardently expected Christ, its creed was of the expectant Christ.

For what it is worth, Dom Gregory Dix has drawn attention to a comparable phenomenon in the liturgical tradition of the Church. From the very beginning, as the *marana tha* prayer indicates, the primitive Eucharist was intensely eschatological. Yet, as Dix pointed out (*The Shape of the Liturgy*, p. 264 f.), it is not till the end of the fourth century[1] that the second coming is mentioned as a separate item in the *anamnesis*, along with the other events of salvation which the Eucharist 're-calls'. And he goes on to comment that this development 'represents not the continuance but the *breakdown* of the primitive conception. . . . The whole notion of the *eschaton* is . . . split into two parts, the one in the historic past and the other in the historic future, instead of both in combination being regarded as a single fact of the eternal present.' The parallel with Professor Cullmann's conclusions from the credal evidence is striking, and it may be that the liturgical tradition, with its notoriously conservative character, is an additional witness that should not be ignored, even for the earliest period.

To the theological significance of all this we shall return. Here we record it merely as part of the evidence that the facts about the *Parousia* hope are not quite as simple as its

---

[1] *Ap. Const.*, viii. It may not be insignificant that this is what Dix calls 'a "made-up" liturgy, a literary production' rather than the direct product of the worshipping community. My attention was drawn to this reference by the Reverend D. M. Paton.

spread throughout the New Testament would suggest. When we come to probe its origins, we seem to reach a stratum where it is puzzlingly conspicuous by its absence. It should again be emphasized that this in itself proves nothing. If it can be shown, as naturally we should assume, that the expectation goes back to Jesus himself, then the fact that traces of it elude us during the twenty years that separate the Crucifixion from Paul's arrival at Thessalonica is of little significance. It is the evidence of the Gospels that is decisive, and to this now we must turn. We have paused to look at what may only be a curious fault in the record of transmission—or may, of course, have other and more interesting import.

JESUS' OWN EXPECTATION:
1. THE HOPE OF GLORY

In the previous chapter we looked at the expectation of Christ's return as we find it in the early Church, and tried to isolate in it what was new from those other elements in the Christian view of the End which were merely taken over from Judaism. We then began the attempt to trace its origin. The Epistles and Acts give no direct answer to that question; and indeed when we carry the search beyond a certain point we find the expectation eluding us in a curious way. But there is one answer which, though nowhere suggested in these documents, would so obviously account for the phenomena, that it must be presumed the most probable until it is proved otherwise. This is that the disciples expected Jesus because he himself had led them to expect him. The expectation of Jesus, the fact that Jesus was expected, leads directly to the question of what Jesus expected. Is the origin of the *Parousia* doctrine to be found in his own teaching? How did he himself view the climax of his work and the end of his mission in the purpose of God?

It is important, again, to spend a little time in isolating the real question that is here at issue. For there is no doubt that Jesus shared with his contemporaries a number of convictions about the End, which he certainly held whether or not he spoke of his own return in glory. Since these things are not in dispute, it will be well to keep them separate in our discussion.

Like every Jew, Jesus looked to the consummation of all things in the final vindication of God and his saints; and he

36

was content to represent it in the traditional picture of the heavenly banquet (Matt. 8.11 f. = Luke 13.28 f.; Luke 14.15–24). Though we cannot be sure that he used the actual expression 'the consummation of the age', which Matthew alone places upon his lips (Matt. 13.39 f., 49; 24.3; 28.20), there is good reason to suppose that he thought, in the current Jewish manner, of the distinction between 'this age' and 'the age to come' (Matt. 12.32; Mark 10.30 = Luke 18.30; Luke 16.8; 20.34 f.). Again, even if 'the end' as a technical term for 'the end of the world' occurs only in somewhat suspect verses (Mark 13.7 and pars.; Matt. 24.14), he certainly made use of the conventional phraseology of heaven and earth passing away (Matt. 5.18 = Luke 16.17; Mark 13.31 and pars). Moreover, like every Jew, Jesus visualized history as bounded by the final judgement,[1] 'that day' of traditional expectation (Matt. 5.21–30; 7.22; 10.15; 11.21–4; 12.36, 41 f.; Luke 10. 12–15; 11.31 f.), which would be marked by a general resurrection (Mark 12.25–7 and pars.; Luke 14.14) and a final separation of saved and lost.[2]

This 'day' lay for him essentially within the Father's sole authority (Acts 1.7; cf. Mark 13.32). Yet at the same time there

[1]I cannot follow Glasson in his denial of this, op. cit., pp. 128–34.
[2]Matt. 8.11 f. = Luke 13.28 f., etc. There are a number of passages in the special Matthean material which treat in some detail of the last judgement and the division it will bring, in particular, the parables of the Tares (13.24–30, 36–43) and the Dragnet (13.47–50) and the vision of the Sheep and the Goats (25.31–46). Matthew is here in all probability reapplying to the Church and to the end of the world the teaching describing originally the division for and against the Kingdom of God which the crisis of the ministry of Jesus must bring (Luke 12.51–3 = Matt. 10. 34–6; cf. Matt. 15.12–14a with Matt. 13.29 f., and *vide* my article, 'The "Parable" of the Sheep and the Goats', *New Testament Studies*, II (1956), pp. 225–37). This does not mean that Jesus did not speak of the last judgement (which from other evidence he clearly did). It means simply that, with the rest of the traditional elements we are considering, his teaching presupposed it rather than expounded it: the *subject* of his preaching was, rather, the eschatological crisis in which men stood *now*.

are passages which leave no doubt that he saw himself as intimately connected with it. It will involve *his* glory, even though the places of honour are not his to dispose (Mark 10.35–40 and par.); the table at the banquet will be not only God's but *his* (Luke 22.30); and above all, he, as Son of man, will be associated with the day of judgement, though, in the earliest strata, not as judge but as advocate and accuser. Men's acceptance or rejection of him now will govern God's acceptance or rejection of them then (Matt. 7.22 f.; 10.32 f.; Luke 12.8 f.; 13.25–7).

The unique position in relation to the final purpose of God in which Jesus thus claimed to stand would present itself to a Jew as near to blasphemy. But in the actual categories of the End we have so far mentioned there was nothing that would not have been common ground, at any rate to every Pharisee. The language itself and the hopes of which it spoke were part of the common stock of Jewish expectation,[1] and require no particular explanation. They remain valid, whether or not Jesus introduced into their framework the thought of his own return. Moreover, like the Church after him, he could have visualized the End in completely Christocentric terms— with his own unique relation to the consummation, the judgement, the resurrection, stressed to the maximum—without this implying of itself that he would come again to earth. As an illustration of this, the Fourth Gospel can ascribe to Jesus such sayings as, 'The word that *I* have spoken will be his judge on the last day' (John 12.48) and '*I* will raise him up at the last day' (6.54), without making any association between this last day and a final *Parousia*.

This has been said again for two reasons. The first is to isolate that element which really does stand in need of explanation, and which we are here concerned to examine. And the second is to emphasize that Jesus' belief in the final consummation of God's purpose is never in question: that is presupposed, whatever other expectation he did or did not

[1] For a convenient catena of parallels, *vide* S. P. T. Prideaux, *The Second Coming of Christ*, ch. I.

entertain. No more in the Gospels than in the Epistles are we necessarily shut up *either* to the *Parousia* hope *or* to a completely realized eschatology, in which no expectation for the future remains.

It was into this accepted framework of Jewish hope that Jesus brought a new announcement. It spoke of a decisive act which God was even now performing and whose climax he described in such terms as the coming in power, whether of the Kingdom of God, or of the Son of man. And it is upon this language that we must concentrate if we are to understand and evaluate the distinctive element in his expectation.

Now this language will be found upon examination to give expression to two closely related and often inseparable ideas, both of which are integrally involved in the conception of the *Parousia*. These are the themes, on the one hand, of *vindication*—of victory out of defeat—and, on the other, of *visitation* —of a coming among men in power and judgement. How easily the one slips over into the other may be illustrated by the minute variation in the text of Luke 23.42. According to one reading, the thief on the cross says to Jesus: 'Remember me when you come *into* your kingdom'. That speaks of vindication, of the King coming to his own in the sense of entering upon his reign. According to another reading, the thief says: 'Remember me when you come *in* your kingdom'. That represents the idea of visitation, of the King coming to his own in the other sense of coming in power to reign among his people.

It will be useful to separate the two themes for clarity of exposition. But it would be entirely false to set one over against the other, or to suggest that one is a valid element and one an invalid. The *Parousia* idea, of its very nature, includes both, not one or the other. The real issue is when and how both of these are seen by Jesus as reaching their fulfilment. When he speaks of 'coming to his own' in either sense, to what does this language refer? Does it point to a moment lying *beyond* the climax of his ministry, and separated from it by an interval; or is he referring to the culmination of his life and ministry itself? In other words, did he, in any sense, visualize a *second* coming, other than that in which he was speaking?

For the remainder of this chapter we shall concentrate upon the theme of vindication, and hold over for the next chapter those sayings which speak of the visitation of the Son of man.

There are a number of words of Jesus pointing to his future vindication which need not detain us long. This is not because they are unimportant—I believe they are decisive—but because there is no dispute about their reference. Thus, there are the three predictions of the Markan narrative (Mark 8.31; 9.31; 10.33 f.; and pars) concerning the rising of the Son of man after suffering and death. There is, of course, room for discussion about the genuineness of these sayings, and some of the more circumstantial details, that he will be delivered to the chief priests and scribes and be mocked and scourged, must almost certainly be discounted as prophecies after the event. There are many who would argue that the whole reference to rising again after three days is suspect, on the grounds that, even if such precise prediction were probable, the attitude of the disciples before or after the Resurrection gives no hint that they had been warned to expect it. But I would agree with Professor R. H. Fuller in his *Mission and Achievement of Jesus* (p. 56) that, even if we delete the specific reference to resurrection, the very use of the term 'the Son of man' implies a figure of glory and vindication, and, if the title be derived from the scene in Daniel 7 (as I believe to be overwhelmingly probable), of vindication through and out of suffering.

But the details of authenticity may here be left on one side. For no one disputes what alone is our concern at the moment, that the reference of these sayings must be to the culmination of the earthly ministry of Jesus. It is of this moment, and not of any second coming, that the vindication is predicted, whatever precisely may have been the language he used.

And there are other sayings which fall at once into the same class. Thus, in the words of Luke 12.50

'I have a baptism to be baptized with; and how I am constrained until it is accomplished!'

it is clear that Jesus is referring to the release and victory that will mark the end of his present obedience, which is involving him now in constriction and ultimately in death.

Very similar is the perhaps deliberately enigmatic saying of Luke 13.32 f.:

'Behold, I cast out demons and perform cures today and tomorrow, and the third day I am perfected. Nevertheless I must go on my way today and tomorrow and the day following; for it cannot be that a prophet should perish away from Jerusalem.'[1]

The moment of consummation of Jesus and his mission, related closely to his death at Jerusalem, is here again clearly seen as the end and climax of the Ministry itself.

Professor Carl Kraeling[2] has given a similar interpretation to the obscure saying of Matt. 11.12:

'From the days of John the Baptist until now the kingdom of heaven is suffering violence and men of violence take it by force.'

This indicates, he thinks, that Jesus visualized three periods in the coming of the Kingdom: (1) the period of preparation, prior to John, of the Law and the Prophets; (2) the present period, up to and including the moment of speaking, when the Kingdom, though operative, is subject to duress and violence (such as has already engulfed John and must eventually overtake Jesus too); and (3) a period of fruition and fulfilment, which lies still in the future. Here, the last stage, the vindication of the Kingdom is merely implied, but it is evidently viewed as supervening upon the end of the opposition to which hitherto it has been exposed.

[1]For the integrity of the saying as it stands, cf. V. Taylor, *Jesus and His Sacrifice,* pp. 170 f.
[2]*John the Baptist,* pp. 156 f.; he is followed by A. N. Wilder, op. cit., p. 149.

Further, and related to the 'baptism' saying of Luke 12.50, there is the other passage, in Mark 10.35–40, in which Jesus speaks of the baptism with which he is baptized (or, strictly, is being baptized). Once more, his triumph, which lies beyond this baptism, is tied in the closest possible way to his suffering and death. There can be no thought of 'glory' except through drinking the cup of death. The one is but the gateway to the other.

With this we may connect sayings at the Last Supper which speak in the same way of a fulfilment out of and immediately beyond the present situation of distress. In words confirmed in part by the independent tradition of Mark 14.25, Jesus says, according to Luke 22.15–18:

' "I have earnestly desired to eat this passover with you before I suffer; for I tell you I shall not eat it until it is fulfilled in the kingdom of God." And he took a cup, and when he had given thanks he said, "Take this, and divide it among yourselves; for I tell you that from now on I shall not drink of the fruit of the vine until the kingdom of God comes".'[1]

And a few verses later, in 22.28–30, Jesus combines the prediction of his own vindication out of suffering with that of his disciples:

'You are those who have continued with me in my trials; as my Father appointed a kingdom for me, so do I appoint for you that you may eat and drink at my table in my kingdom, and sit on thrones judging the twelve tribes of Israel.'

With this, finally, we may compare Luke 12.32:

'Fear not, little flock, for it is your Father's good pleasure to give you the kingdom.'

[1] Kümmel (op. cit., pp. 32, 37, 77) argues that this saying presupposes a lapse of time between Jesus' death and the coming of the Kingdom. But there is no more necessity to identify 'that day' when Jesus will drink the new wine (Mark 14.25) with the final Day of Judgement than there is to do so in Mark 2.20, where 'that day' when the disciples will fast is clearly the moment of Jesus' departure from them.

This saying, like one we are about to examine, may well, as Dr Glasson suggests (op. cit., p. 53), recall by its wording the classic scene of vindication in Daniel 7, where in v. 27 the saints of the Most High, after being worn out by intimidation and oppression, are 'given the kingdom' by God.

In each of these cases we have the thought of a vindication out of present tribulation, in the first instance of Jesus himself, but also of his own, which is linked to the imminent climax of the historic ministry of Jesus. This is to be the point of entry upon his reign. There is no suggestion in any of these sayings, which together form an impressive testimony, of any moment other than or separate from this climax, at once of deepest humiliation by man and of most certain vindication by God.

We turn now to a saying which I believe to be connected closely with those we have considered, and indeed to be the most decisive of them all. This is the solemn adjuration at the trial of Jesus (Matt. 26.64; Mark 14.62; Luke 22.69), which, according to our first three Gospels, finally sealed his fate with the Jews. It will be necessary to examine it in some detail, since upon its interpretation a good deal hangs. It is in fact the one of the five texts adduced by von Hügel that Canon Fison allows as a basis for the *Parousia* expectation on the lips of Jesus;[1] and earlier Dr Dodd wrote in his *Parables of the Kingdom* (p. 96): 'It is doubtful . . . whether the earlier tradition contained explicit predictions of the second coming of Jesus as Son of man, apart from Mark 14.62.'[2]

According to Mark, whose version, on the generally established principles of New Testament criticism, we must start by taking as the most original, Jesus replied to the High Priest's challenge, 'Are you the Christ, the Son of the Blessed?', with the words:

[1] *Vide* p. 11 above.

[2] Dr Dodd tells me that he also would now interpret the saying along the lines given below. For the authenticity of this saying cf. Dodd, op. cit., p. 91 n. 1; V. Taylor, *St Mark*, ad loc.; Kümmel, op. cit., p. 50 and the authorities there cited.

'I am; and you will see the Son of man sitting at the right hand of Power, and coming with the clouds of heaven.'

Jesus' answer contains an echo of two Scriptural passages, whose meaning would not be lost upon his audience. The first is Ps. 110.1, which, according to Mark 12.36, he had recently used to some effect against the Scribes:

'The Lord said to my Lord, "Sit at my right hand, till I put thy enemies under thy feet".'

This speaks of a verdict of vindication pronounced by God and a promise to his servant of triumph out of the power of his enemies. In saying that his adversaries will see the Son of man sitting at the right hand of Power, Jesus is clearly claiming that God is going to vindicate him by a similar act of crowning deliverance.

The second half of his statement, that the Son of man would come with the clouds of heaven, contains an even clearer allusion to Dan. 7.13:

'I saw in the night visions, and behold, with the clouds of heaven there came one like a son of man, and he came to the Ancient of Days and was presented before him.'

Now this also, and the entire chapter from which it comes, is, as we have already said, a classic passage of vindication. In the vision, the figure of a man, representing, after the beastlike figures of the four world empires, 'the saints of the Most High', is brought out of humiliation and defeat to the judgement seat of God, there to be 'given judgement' and receive 'the dominion and the greatness of the kingdom under the whole heaven'.

There could hardly be a setting more dramatically appropriate for Jesus' reference. At the very moment when his enemies have finally 'prevailed' over him and set up their court to condemn him, Jesus declares that 'the time has come for judgment to be given' not for them, but for 'the saints of the Most High', who, embodied in his own person as Son of man, are now to 'receive the kingdom' (Dan. 7.22). For out of suffering and death he is about to be brought in triumph to the throne of God, in a crowning act of vindication which they themselves will witness.

If this passage stood by itself, there could, I think, be no doubt that such was Jesus' meaning when he combined these words of Daniel with the opening verse of the Coronation Psalm. There is every presumption, till we have reason to think otherwise, that he understood them in the sense in which they were written, and, as far as we know, had always been understood, to speak of a coming *to* God in ascent and vindication. 'It cannot be too strongly emphasized', Professor T. W. Manson has said,[1] 'that what Daniel portrays is not a divine, semi-divine, or angelic figure coming down from heaven, to bring deliverance, but a human figure going up to heaven to receive it'. And the context in which Jesus makes the allusion fits this meaning like a glove. In other words, the two predictions of 'sitting at the right hand of God' and 'coming on the clouds of heaven' are to be understood as parallel expressions, static and dynamic, for the same conviction. Jesus is not at this point speaking of a coming *from* God: in whatever other sayings he may refer to the coming of the Son of man in visitation, here at any rate he is affirming his vindication.[2]

[1]'The Son of man in Daniel, Enoch and the Gospels', *Bulletin of the John Rylands Library,* XXXII (1950), p. 174; cf. E. W. Heaton, *The Book of Daniel* (Torch Commentary), ad loc.

[2]The history of this interpretation (strongly argued by Glasson, op. cit., pp. 63–8 and accepted by V. Taylor, *St Mark*, ad loc.) is sketched by Beasley-Murray, op. cit., p. 259. His attempt to discredit it is unconvincing. The important point is not whether in Daniel the scene is laid in heaven or earth: the locus of an apocalyptic vision, like that of a dream, is, literally, neither here nor there. What is indisputable is that it is a scene of vindication and that the Son of man comes *to* the Ancient of Days. Nor, as others have argued (e.g. Fison, op. cit., pp. 192 f.), can the order of the two quotations (that the Son of man first sits and then comes) be regarded as decisive. The interpretation subsequently given to the saying by the Evangelist would in any case impose this order; if they were originally parallel expressions, their sequence would have been indifferent.

Moreover, the impression that Mark leaves upon us is one of *imminent* vindication: the Sanhedrin is about to witness a dramatic reversal of judgement, such as Daniel pictures with the intervention of God. No time is specified; but it would be natural to assume, as must inevitably be assumed of the session at God's right hand, that Jesus is here referring to the same moment of vindication out of suffering which earlier he had described, when not in the context of the law-court, in language reminiscent rather of the suffering Servant, whose divine destiny also was to 'be exalted and lifted up and be very high' (Isa. 52.13). The saying at the Trial would then simply take up, and crown, those previous prophecies of the vindication of the Son of man which sound like a knell through the second half of St Mark's Gospel:

'The Son of man will be delivered into the hands of men, and they will kill him; and when he is killed, after three days he will rise.'[1]

This, from Mark 9.31, is the version showing least sign of embellishment, and in it the phrase, 'after three days', if not written in later, is to be taken as an expression for *speedy* restoration, such as is promised to Israel in Hos. 6.2:

'After two days he will revive us;
and on the third day he will raise us up,
that we may live before him.'[2]

The natural supposition, that is to say, from Mark's account is that Jesus was speaking at his trial of an immediate vindication of himself and his cause, out of the very jaws of humiliation and defeat. In Dr G. S. Duncan's words, 'When

---

[1]Cf. A. Schweitzer, *The Quest of the Historical Jesus*, p. 364 n. 1: 'If, therefore, Jesus . . . predicted to his disciples his resurrection, he means by that, not a single isolated act, but a complex occurrence consisting of his metamorphosis, translation to heaven, and *Parousia* as the Son of man . . . It is, therefore, one and the same thing whether he speaks of his resurrection or of his coming on the clouds of heaven.'

[2]Cf. Dodd, op. cit., pp. 99 f., 103.

. . . Jesus makes his bold declaration to the supreme representatives of the earthly powers which are about to condemn him, the conviction that floods his soul is, not that at some undefined future date he will return to execute judgment, but rather that here and now he is being invested with permanent authority as God's supreme representative among men' (*Jesus, Son of Man*, p. 176).

If, with this in mind, we turn to the Matthean and Lucan versions of this saying, we are struck at once by the fact that in each of them there is introduced a qualifying phrase, putting beyond doubt that what they describe is to take place 'from this moment'. In Matt. 26.64 it is: 'From now on[1] you will see the Son of man sitting at the right hand of Power, and coming on the clouds of heaven'; and in Luke 22.69: 'From now on[2] the Son of man shall be seated at the right hand of the power of God'. This concurrence between the two Evangelists is remarkable, if both are using Mark and working independently; and it is made the more interesting by the fact that this same verse contains two further agreements of Matthew and Luke over against Mark. Both record an evasive rather than a direct answer to the question, 'Are you the Christ?';[3] and both have a 'but' between the two halves of Jesus' reply, where Mark has a simple 'and'. The sense then becomes: 'Are you the Christ?' 'That is your term. But what

[1] ἀπ' ἄρτι. With Oepke (op. cit., *T.W.N.T.*, V, 865), I cannot accept A. Debrunner's thesis (*Coniectanea Neotestamentica*, XI, p. 48) that ἀπαρτί [*sic*] here and elsewhere means 'assuredly', though granting that it may be the correct interpretation of Rev. 14.13. .

[2] ἀπὸ τοῦ νῦν.

[3] Since all the Evangelists, including Mark, later agree on an indirect reply to Pilate (σὺ λέγεις; Mark 15.2 and pars.), the 'I am' of Mark 14.62 is unique in the Gospels. E. J. Goodspeed's attempt (*Problems of N.T. Translation*, pp. 64–8) to make the σὺ εἶπας of Matt. 26.64 represent an unequivocal 'Yes' and his πλήν mean 'furthermore' (a sense unparalleled in the New Testament) stems from an *a priori* conviction that Matthew *could* not be weakening Mark. The conviction is sound but the conclusion precarious. Cf. M. Smith, 'Notes on Goodspeed's "Problems of N.T. Translation",' *Journal of Biblical Literature*, LXIV (1945), pp. 506–10.

you will see, and see at once, is the vindication of the Son of man'.

The last agreement is perhaps of minor significance, though I believe it represents an authentic countering of the messianic categories in which others wish to see Jesus by his own preference for 'the Son of man'. It is the same in what we have argued to be the closely parallel scene at Caesarea Philippi (Mark 8.29–31). Peter's confession, 'You are the Christ', must at once be recast in terms of 'the Son of man',[1] a title whose associations are with victory only out of suffering. Earlier the emphasis fell on the necessity of the suffering: at the Trial, where this is self-evident, it is on the certainty of the vindication.

But how are we to explain these agreements? There is clearly no later assimilation of the text from one Gospel to the other, as the actual wording in the Greek is different at each point. That both independently are altering Mark is twice as difficult as the supposition that Matthew is here altering Mark. And this I regard as frankly impossible. I cannot believe that Matthew, at the time at which he was writing, could have any conceivable motive in deliberately making ambiguous an unequivocal claim by Jesus to be the Christ. It is the very title round which his Gospel is written, and when Peter attributes it to Jesus at Caesarea Philippi it is he alone who records it as received with approbation. Equally, I cannot believe that Matthew, whose every tendency in matters of eschatology is, as we shall see, towards a futurist apocalyptic, should deliberately have added to Mark a phrase that would make the coming of Jesus on the clouds into an event occurring from the very moment of the Passion; for he has spent the whole of the two previous chapters picturing it as happening only at 'the consummation of the age'. That he should have retained the phrase 'from now on' if he had found it in Mark is just credible; for Matthew is more of a collector than a consistent

[1] Cf. the same transition in John 12.34: 'The crowd answered him, "We have heard from the law that *the Christ* remains for ever, and how is that it *you* say that *the Son of man* must be lifted up?" '

theologian, and a number of unresolved conceptions lie together in his Gospel.[1]

But, if he did not modify the confession nor add the 'henceforth', what is the alternative? Can it be that these stood originally in Mark much as Matthew now has them? There is in fact some evidence to suggest that this is so. The textual support for the variants is, to be sure, insufficient to establish the case by itself. But with all the other considerations, it is, I believe, probable that Mark may originally have written:

'*You have said that* I am; *but from now on* you will see the Son of man sitting at the right hand of Power, and coming with the clouds of heaven.'[2]

If so, all that Matthew has then done is to copy Mark, pruning his style, as his custom is, by cutting the cumbersome phrase 'You have said that I am' to 'You have said'.

This gives a perfectly rational explanation of how Matthew comes to have what he has. And there are obvious reasons why in the text of Mark the messianic claim should later have been rendered unambiguous, and, by the simple omission of 'from now on', the words about coming on the clouds have been brought into line with the prediction of the previous chapter (13.26) that it is only at the End that the Son of man will be seen coming in glory.

The question of Luke's version is complicated by the fact that all through his Passion narrative we cannot be sure

[1]E.g. 10.23; 24.30 and 28.20. Despite his disclaimer, it is surely 'subtilité excessive' to say, with M-J. Lagrange (*S. Matthieu*, pp. clxv f.), that Matthew portrays two quite distinct comings of the Son of man in 26.64 and 24.30, the one of enthronement, the other of consummation. There is not the slightest hint that the apocalyptic *Parousia* of 24.30 is not the same as that predicted at the Trial, nor any suggestion that 10.23 is to be referred to a different and earlier moment, say, than 16.27. Cf. Kümmel, op. cit., p. 67.

[2]σὺ εἶπας ὅτι, is read by Θ, 067, fam. 13, 472, 543, 565, 700, 1071; geo., arm.; Or. ἀπ' ἄρτι is represented in sy[s] and sa (1 ms.). The case for the former is accepted by V. Taylor (op. cit., ad loc.); that for the latter is argued in detail by Glasson (op. cit., pp. 66–8).

whether he is copying Mark or using a tradition of his own.
In fact, at this point he appears to be doing both, reproducing
two replies of Jesus to two questions about his messiahship.
The first, 'If I tell you, you will not believe; and if I ask you,
you will not answer' (22.67 f.), seems to come from a tradition
also represented in the fourth Gospel.[1] The second, 'You
say that I am' (22.70), comes, I suggest, from Mark, and corro-
borates the argument that this is what Mark originally had. In
the matter that immediately concerns us, I believe that Luke
like Matthew has derived his 'henceforth' from Mark, chang-
ing the Greek phrase in accord with his regular stylistic preference.[2] His marked omission of the coming on the clouds,
confining Jesus' prophecy simply to the session at God's
right hand, merely reveals him as a consistent theologian,
since for him the enthronement of Christ did indeed take
place from the Resurrection onwards, but his coming is
reserved for the future. This again I believe to be a credible
account of Luke's text. But wherever he derived his 'henceforth', the conclusion is the same. Either it stood in Mark, or
he took it from another source, which is then independent
evidence for a tradition that Jesus used some such expression.

But, whether or not Jesus thus put the matter beyond
doubt, it seems clear that what he was asserting, and what even
our present text of Mark implies, was the *immediate* vindication of his person and cause. In any case, what is most important is what, I believe, is most certain: that we have here a
saying not of visitation from God but of vindication to God.

What is important is not that 'the coming on the clouds'
means an ascent rather than a descent. This aspect is not
stressed either in Daniel or in the saying of Jesus, though
Daniel leaves no doubt that it is a coming to God.[3] Such

[1]John 10.24 f.: ' "If you are the Christ, tell us plainly". Jesus
answered them, "I told you, and you do not believe". '

[2]Luke never uses ἀπ' ἄρτι, Matthew never ἀπὸ τοῦ νῦν.

[3]In I Enoch 14.8, which is either the inspiration (Glasson, op. cit.,
pp. 14–18, following Charles) or an imitation (H. H. Rowley, *The*

spatial terms are in any case only an accommodation of language, and it is finally of no significance whether man is conceived as coming to God or God coming to man.[1] The importance is that, if this is a saying of vindication, then there can be no doubt that it refers to the only moment to which all the enthronement language applied to Jesus does refer, namely, to the moment of the Resurrection onwards; for there is never a suggestion that Jesus enters upon his triumph only at some *second* coming. If, on the other hand, it is language of visitation, then for us, as for important strands of the New Testament, its reference is to say the least ambiguous. We naturally then associate it with another still future moment, as does the Apostles' Creed when it actually introduces a change of tense between the 'sitting' and the 'coming'. And how deep is the influence of liturgical repetition is plain when so good an exegete as Professor O. Cullmann can write: 'In his answer to the high priest, Jesus distinguishes between the moment when the Son of man will sit at the right hand of God and the one when he will come again on the clouds of heaven' (*Peter: Disciple, Apostle and Martyr*, p. 201). In fact, of course, he does nothing of the sort.

Relevance of Apocalyptic, pp. 75–9) of the scene in Dan. 7.13, the idea of ascent is unambiguous: 'Behold, in the vision clouds invited me . . . and the winds in the vision caused me to fly and lifted me upward, and bore me into heaven'. As evidence of how, later, it was clearly understood in terms of ascent, cf. IV Ezra 13.3: 'And I beheld, and lo! the wind caused to come up out of the heart of the seas as it were the form of a man. And I beheld, and lo! this Man flew with the clouds of heaven.' Glasson points out (op. cit., p.18) that Daniel 7.13 f. was still quoted by Cyprian (*Testimonies* ii, 26) under the heading, 'That after he had risen again he should receive from his Father all power, and his power should be everlasting' and that it has been read continuously in the Church of England as one of the lessons for Ascension Day.

[1]Thus in Daniel 7 itself we have both representations: 'There came one like a son of man, and he came to the Ancient of Days' (v. 13) and, 'Until the Ancient of Days came, and judgement was given for the saints of the Most High' (v. 22).

We said that if this saying at the Trial stood by itself there could be little room for dispute about its meaning. But it does not stand by itself; and it is largely the exegesis of *other* passages which has determined its interpretation. These are texts which do speak, implicitly or explicitly, of a coming in glory from heaven, and they must clearly be taken carefully into account.

There is no doubt that the early Church did expect a descent of Jesus on clouds from heaven,[1] and that the Synoptic Evangelists shared that belief. It should therefore cause no surprise to find reflections of it in the Gospels. Indeed, what is remarkable is that the Evangelists should still preserve traces of a different conception, which evidently they did not share. The only question is whether those texts which do reflect their own expectation represent *merely* the thinking of the Church or that of Jesus as well. In other words, are these passages also to be seen as authentic sayings of Jesus, revealing that he himself thought of the Son of man's coming in glory, not only as one of imminent vindication, but also as a future descent? Granted that there was a second conception, at what stage did it enter the tradition—with Jesus or in the course of subsequent transmission?

There are, indeed, some sayings which speak of a coming in glory that may be attributed without hesitation to the work of the Church. Thus, Matt. 24.3,

'Tell us, when will this be, and what will be the sign of your coming and of the close of the age?',

is quite clearly secondary to Mark 13.4:

'Tell us, when will this be, and what will be the sign when these things [i.e., the destruction of the Temple] are all to be accomplished?'

[1]Cf., e.g., I Thess. 4.16 f.; Acts 1.11. W. K. Lowther Clarke's attempt in his article, 'The Clouds of Heaven', *Theology*, XXXI (1935), pp. 63–72, 128–41 (reprinted in *Divine Humanity*, pp. 9–40), to argue that it was not till the second century that this language was referred to a coming *from* heaven involves far too much special pleading.

Again, Matt. 16.28,

'Truly, I say to you, there are some standing here who will not taste death before they see the Son of man coming in his kingdom,'

is evidently dependent upon Mark 9.1, which contains no reference to the coming of the Son of man.[1] Similarly, Matt.19.28 (contrast Luke 22.28-30),

'Truly, I say to you, in the new world, when the Son of man shall sit on his glorious throne,'

and Matt. 25.31,

'When the Son of man comes in his glory, and all the angels with him, then he will sit on his glorious throne,'

are both, I believe, demonstrably editorial introductions supplied by the Evangelist, rather than words of Jesus.[2]

But there are two other sayings which must be considered at greater length.

The first is that of Mark 8.38:

'For whoever is ashamed of me and of mine[3] in this adulterous and sinful generation, of him will the Son of man also be ashamed, when he comes in the glory of his Father with the holy angels.'

---

[1] Another example of this process is, as Glasson suggests (op. cit., p. 75), probably to be seen in the textual transmission of Luke 23.42, of which mention was made earlier. There are three readings:

(a) when you come into your kingdom (B, L, c, e, f, ff^2, l, r^1, vg)
(b) when you come in your kingdom (most other mss.)
(c) in the day of your coming (D)

The latter two expressions—the reference to Jesus 'coming in his kingdom' and to 'your coming'—we have just seen to be secondary in the only other passages in which they occur (Matt. 16.28 and 24.3). There are good grounds therefore for thinking (a) to be the original reading and for supposing that an allusion to a future coming is here again being created out of a saying of vindication and enthronement.

[2] For the detailed linguistic evidence, cf. again my article, 'The "Parable" of the Sheep and the Goats', *New Testament Studies,* II (1956), pp. 226-9.

[3] λόγους is probably to be omitted, with W, k and sa.

There is nothing in this saying to prevent its being interpreted in the same sense as that at the Trial, namely, of the entry of the Son of man upon the heavenly glory of God. And this I should accept as its original meaning (whatever it may have meant for Mark and the other Evangelists), if I were convinced that Jesus spoke here of such a coming. But it is, I believe, more likely—and Dr Vincent Taylor comes to a similar conclusion (*St Mark*, ad loc.)—that this last clause was added in the course of transmission. For the saying is also represented in the 'Q' tradition (Matt. 10.32 f. = Luke 12.8 f.), but there without reference to a coming in glory. In its Lucan, and almost certainly more original[1] form, it runs:

'Every one who acknowledges me before men, the Son of man also will acknowledge before the angels of God; but he who denies me before men will be denied before the angels of God.'

As Dr Glasson says (op. cit., p. 75), it is hard to think of any reason why the community tradition should have reduced the version of Mark 8.38 to what stands in the other source. On the other hand, there are, as we have seen, instances enough— and one of them in the very next verse (Mark 9.1 = Matt. 16.28)—of the reverse process, of *Parousia* sayings created by the Church out of ones that originally contained no reference to it; and this must be regarded as yet a further example. This particular passage, indeed, with its Synoptic parallels provides a specially striking instance of a well-recognizable pattern of development to which we shall return later (pp. 93 f. below). But, general tendencies apart, there are two further reasons for suspecting the Markan phrase, 'when he comes in the glory of his Father'.

In the first place, it represents God as the Father of the Son of man (equating, by implication, the titles 'Son of man' and 'Son of God'), in a manner unparalleled either in Jewish

---

[1]Matthew has cut out the reference to the Son of man (common to both the Markan and Q versions), as appearing to throw doubt on his identity with Jesus. N.b. too his characteristic phrase: 'my Father who is in heaven'.

usage or in that of primitive Christianity.[1] Of course, for the Church, God is the Father of Jesus and Jesus is the Son of man; but the use of the phrase evidently reflects a stage of development when 'the Son of man' is losing its significance as a title and becoming, like the term 'Christ', simply a proper name for Jesus.

And, secondly, the idea of the Son of man 'coming' in judgement belongs to a conception in which the Son of man is himself the judge. According to the earlier tradition, represented by the saying as we have it in 'Q' (and indeed in the body of Mark 8.38), as well as in Matt. 7.22 f. = Luke 13.26 f., Jesus pictures himself as occupying the Old Testament rôle[2] of the figure who stands at the judgement before the throne of God to accuse or to plead for those he represents. This, Jesus' own understanding of his function, is probably still reflected in Acts 7.56,[3] where Stephen sees him as the Son of man *standing* at the right hand of God, that is to say, as his advocate in the judgement with his enemies.[4] But the general position of the Church was that by virtue of the Resurrection Jesus was himself designated *judge* on God's behalf (Acts 10.42; 17.31). Consequently, in the later strands of the Gospel tradition, he is made to occupy the throne of judgement itself (Matt. 19.28; 25.31). And, in this capacity as judge, it is natural that he should also be represented as 'coming' (as, again, in Matt. 25.31); for in the Biblical tradition God regularly 'comes' to judge the world (e.g. Pss. 96.13; 98.9; Dan. 7.22; I Enoch 3.9). The fact therefore that in Mark 8.38b the Son of man is envisaged as coming in

[1]The only other instance, apart from the parallels to this verse (Matt. 16.27; Luke 9.26, where Luke has '*the* Father') occurs in Matt. 25.34. Here the phrase 'of my Father' (and with it the whole equation of 'the King' and 'the Son of man') is, I have tried to show, Matthew's own editorial work (*vide*, op. cit., *N.T. Studies*, II, 229 f.).

[2]Cf. I Kings 22.19–22; Job. 16.19; 19.25; Zech. 3.1–5.

[3]Also in II Tim. 2.12 and Rev. 3.5; cf. Heb. 7.25; 9.24.

[4]*Vide* C. F. D. Moule, 'From Defendant to Judge—and Deliverer,' *Studiorum Novi Testamenti Societas*, Bulletin III (1954), pp. 46 f.

judgement[1] suggests that a different conception of his function has been imposed upon the original saying; and this change has become quite explicit in the Matthean version (16.27), where he is no longer the advocate at all but 'comes . . . to repay every man for what he has done'.

It looks, then, as if the concluding phrase of the Markan version, 'when he comes in the glory of his Father with the holy angels', cannot safely be regarded as belonging to the original words of Jesus. In any case, it cannot be allowed to determine, let alone to controvert, the interpretation of the Trial saying.

The other, and sole remaining, passage in the Gospels to speak of the coming of the Son of man in glory is that which has exercised more influence than any in determining the understanding of Jesus' words; and indeed it must be decisive for interpreting the intention of the Evangelists. It is the prediction which forms the climax of the apocalypse or vision of the End in Mark 13.26 and parallels:

'And then they will see the Son of man coming in clouds with great power and glory.'

We cannot at this point enter into the question of the structure and authenticity of this perplexing discourse. That will come up for consideration later, in chapter VI. It undoubtedly contains much genuine tradition of the teaching of Jesus. But, however much the various reconstructions may disagree among themselves,[2] there is virtual unanimity that, if later composition is to be found in the chapter at all, it is in the paragraph in which these words occur. This section (Mark 13.24–7) is a pastiche of Old Testament allusions, to which Matthew and Luke in their turn have added.[3] In one of

---

[1] If that indeed is the meaning, and not that of Mark 14.62, where the Son of man comes to the judgement throne himself to be vindicated.

[2] For an exhaustive survey, *vide* Beasley-Murray, op. cit.

[3] With Mark 13.24 cf. Isa. 13.10; Ezek. 32.7 f.; etc. 25; v. cf. Isa. 34.4; v 26 cf. Dan. 7.13; v 27 cf. Zech. 2.6; Deut. 30.4; etc.; with Matt. 24.30 cf. Isa. 11.12; Zech. 12.12–14; v 31 cf. Isa. 27.13; with Luke 21.25 cf. Ps. 65.7.

these, a clear echo of Zech. 2.6, the point of the allusion depends entirely on its being taken from the Greek translation,[1] a fact fatally damaging to the view that Jesus himself is quoting. In any case, the entire mosaic is quite untypical of how Jesus elsewhere uses Scripture. But it is exactly how we know the Church proceeded when it turned its hand to composing apocalypses; for II Thess. 1.8–10, which we shall examine later, represents a patchwork of precisely the same kind. The inclusion among these Scriptural allusions of Dan. 7.13, with its reference to the Son of man coming on the clouds, is doubtless due to the fact that Jesus was remembered to have quoted it.[2] But the whole impression of these verses is of a secondary compilation on which it is impossible to rely for any fresh light on how Jesus himself thought.[3]

The conclusion then must be that the other sayings using language similar to that at the Trial cannot be accepted as primary or independent evidence for interpreting the mind of Jesus. As far as his own words are concerned, there is nothing to suggest that he shared the expectation of a return in glory which the Church entertained and ascribed to him. Such language appears for him, rather, to have been another expression of the assurance, reflected in so many of his sayings, that the hour of his vindication was at hand, when, through and out of his present sufferings, God would inaugurate

[1]LXX: 'From the four winds of heaven will I gather you'; Heb.: 'I have spread you abroad as the four winds of heaven.' Cf. Glasson, op. cit., p. 187, who shows that in the allusion to Isa. 34.4 the reference to 'the powers of the heavens' and the 'stars falling' also depends on the LXX version.

[2]If something like Mark 14.62 is not authentic, then it is hard to see how it entered the tradition; for the complete absence of the term from the Epistles shows that the Church itself had no theology of the Son of man.

[3]Cf. Taylor, op. cit., ad loc.: 'This section . . . must be judged as an apocalyptic writing rather than a spoken discourse. It is highly doubtful therefore if v. 26 can be regarded as an actual saying of Jesus'. So also Kümmel, op. cit., pp. 102–4, who shows no tendency to dispose lightly of *Parousia* sayings. For further evidence of the secondary character of these verses, *vide* pp. 118–20 below.

his kingdom in power. Whether that hope was stated in terms of his release from present constraint (Luke 12.50), his perfecting (Luke 13.32), his rising again (Mark 8.31; 9.9, 31; 10.33 f.), his session at the right hand of power (Mark 14.62), his entry upon his kingdom (Luke 23.42) and his glory (Luke 24.26; cf. Mark 10.37), or whether it was framed in terms of his coming with the clouds of heaven (Mark 14.62), the meaning and the reference was the same. It was to that moment when everything for which he and his followers stood would be fulfilled in the kingdom of God (Luke 22.16; cf. 22.28–30; 12.32) and in the inauguration thenceforward of the new covenant through his blood (Luke 22.20; Mark 14.24).

'Will not God vindicate his elect who cry to him day and night? Will he delay long over them? I tell you, he will vindicate them speedily' (Luke 18.7 f.; cf. 23.42 f.).

Such was the promise that Jesus held out. There would indeed be a *Parousia*, in the sense of a coming to appear before the presence of God, and it would be inaugurated 'henceforth' (Matt. 26.64; Luke 22.69), through his own redemptive death. In this its aspect of vindication, Jesus' language requires for its focus no second or subsequent moment. That, to be sure, has always been admitted. Though it may have been divided between the Resurrection and Ascension, it has never ceased to be associated with this complex of events. All that here is open to dispute is how much of his language is really language of vindication.

But what of the other aspect? The passage just cited continues:

'I tell you, he will vindicate them speedily. Nevertheless, when the Son of man comes, will he find faith on earth?' (Luke 18.8.)

This last is typical of the other class of sayings, those which speak of a coming in visitation. To these we must now turn our attention. And here we shall find that the area of dispute is appreciably wider.

JESUS' OWN EXPECTATION:
2. THE COMING CRISIS

THAT God would 'visit' his people in preparation for 'the great and terrible day of the Lord' was a hope deeply rooted in the expectation of the Jews.

'Behold, I send my messenger to prepare the way before me, and the Lord whom you seek will suddenly come to his temple; the messenger of the covenant in whom you delight, behold, he is coming, says the Lord of hosts. But who can endure the day of his coming, and who can stand when he appears?' (Mal. 3.1 f.)

There can be no doubt that Jesus set his own 'coming' in the light of such expectations. The whole of his ministry, and particularly its climax, was seen by him, one could almost say staged by him, as a deliberate coming of the representative of God to his people. This found its symbolic and culminating expression in the triumphal entry into Jerusalem, when the crowds welcomed Jesus, as they were no doubt intended to welcome him, as the one 'who comes in the name of the Lord' (Mark 11.9 and pars.). And closely associated with this in the first three Gospels (Mark 11.15–17 and pars.) is the cleansing of the Temple, in fulfilment of the words of Malachi that the Lord in his messenger would 'come to his temple' to 'purify the sons of Levi and refine them like gold and silver, till they present right offerings to the Lord' (Mal. 3.1–3).

The moral of these acts of prophetic symbolism should have been clear. This was for Jerusalem the day of her visitation. Yet she knew it not (Luke 19.44). And so Jesus drove home their meaning by a story, about tenant farmers left in charge of a vineyard (Mark 12.1–12 and pars.). Of all the parables, this is the one of which perhaps we may say with most confidence that it is preserved in its original setting. In each of the Synoptic Gospels it stands alone and in the same place, not absorbed into a collection,[1] but preserved as part of the situation to which it is so tellingly addressed. Even if its details may have been pointed up by allegorization, its teaching is unmistakable: Jesus comes to his people, as God's final and unique representative, demanding the fruits of their entire history of grace and opportunity. This is the moment when the reckoning must be made, when the whole of Israel's past is to be required. All turns on whether this last emissary is accepted and God's requirement is met: if not, then the moment of visitation becomes the moment of dispossession and rejection.

That such is the place and hour in God's dealings with Israel in which Jesus viewed his coming is confirmed by another passage, this time in the material common to Matthew and Luke (Matt. 23.34–8 = Luke 11.49–51 and 13.34–5a). In the version given by Luke, which is almost certainly the more original,[2] Jesus sums up his attack on the Jewish leaders in the manner of the Prophets, and, for the only time in his recorded utterances, may deliberately be adopting a style of address corresponding to their 'Thus saith the Lord!'

'For this reason also God in his wisdom has said, "I will send them prophets and messengers, some of whom they will kill and persecute", that the blood of all the prophets, shed from the foundation of the world, may be required of this generation, from the blood of Abel to the blood of Zechariah, who perished between the altar and the sanctuary. Yes, I tell you, it shall be required of this generation.'

[1]Matthew has indeed preceded it by another parable about a vineyard (21.28–31), but it is this which is quite evidently the insertion.

[2]For an admirable discussion and interpretation of the passage, *vide* T. W. Manson, *The Sayings of Jesus*, pp. 238 f. Matthew refers the whole utterance to the treatment *still to be accorded* to the emissaries of the Christian Church.

Speaking as the interpreter of the divine wisdom, Jesus sketches the history of God's dealing with Israel, exactly as in the parable of the Wicked Husbandmen, and concludes with the same warning to his contemporaries, that it is upon them that the reckoning now has come.

He then goes on, in a passage which Luke has detached,[1] but where he continues, I think, to speak in the name of God:[2]

'O Jerusalem, Jerusalem, killing the prophets and stoning them who are sent to you! How often would I have gathered your children together as a hen gathers her brood under her wings, and you would not! Behold, your house is forsaken.'

[1]It is all 'Q' material, but Luke separates the address to the City and makes it a comment on the saying from his own source in 13.33: 'It cannot be that a prophet should perish away from Jerusalem'. His reason for this may have been to present the closing words of all, 'I tell you, you will not see me until you say, "Blessed be he who comes in the name of the Lord" ' (Luke 13.35b), as a prediction of the Triumphal Entry. In Matthew they come where all the rest of the passage most naturally belongs (cf. Luke 19.41–4) *after* the Entry, and they must therefore be referred to the *Parousia*. But though this closing saying was already attached in the Evangelist's source to the apostrophe of Jerusalem, strong reasons can be advanced for thinking that it was originally spoken on a separate and previous occasion (cf. Glasson, op. cit., pp. 100–3). It must be interpreted on its own merits, and the interpretation Luke gives is as good as any. It is a pity that he did not simply detach the saying itself, instead of the previous verse and a half as well, in order to give it.

[2]Cf. Glasson, op. cit., pp. 99–101. As evidence, if no more, of how the passage was taken, cf. IV Ezra 1.28–33, where very similar words are ascribed to God: 'Thus saith the Lord Almighty . . . I gathered you together, as a hen gathereth her chickens under her wings: but now, what shall I do unto you? . . . I sent you my servants the prophets, whom you have slain, and torn their bodies in pieces, whose blood I will require of your hands, saith the Lord. Thus saith the Lord Almighty, Your house is desolate, I will cast you out as the wind doth stubble'. For the image of the bird applied to God's protection of his people, cf. Deut. 32.10 f., Ps. 91.4; Isa. 31.5.

It is still God addressing his people, just as in the past he had spoken through his prophets, and in particular Jeremiah:

'I have persistently sent all my servants the prophets to them, day after day; yet they did not listen to me, or incline their ear, but stiffened their neck. They did worse than their fathers (Jer. 7.25 f.).

And again:

'You have neither listened nor inclined your ears to hear, although the Lord persistently sent to you all his servants the prophets' (25.4).

And after both these sayings Jeremiah proceeds to predict the desolation of Jerusalem, describing it again in words of God which Jesus echoed:

'I have forsaken my house,
    I have abandoned my heritage;
I have given the beloved of my soul
    into the hands of her enemies' (12.7).

And just as Jeremiah said,

'The days are coming, says the Lord, when . . . I will make to cease from the cities of Judah and from the streets of Jerusalem the voice of mirth and the voice of gladness . . . for the land shall become a waste' (7.32–4);

and

'In the time of their visitation they shall be cast down, says the Lord' (8.12),

so Jesus was to weep over the City, and say,

'The days shall come upon you, when your enemies will cast up a bank about you and surround you, and hem you in on every side, and dash you to the ground, you and your children within you, and they will not leave one stone upon another in you; because you did not know the time of your visitation' (Luke 19.41–4).

The day of Jerusalem's visitation had arrived: his own ministry was that coming of God to his people to which all along their history had been leading and in which now finally their responsibility was focused. Such, inescapably, is the conclusion of these passages, and it is in their light that we must examine the rest of the teaching of Jesus about the coming of the Son of man.

First, we may note the number of Jesus' sayings which speak of the significance of that coming in the past tense— what might be called the great 'I cames', corresponding to the 'I ams' of the Fourth Gospel.

'I came to cast fire upon the earth; and would that it were already kindled!' (Luke 12.49).

'Do not think that I came to bring peace on earth; I came not to bring peace but a sword' (Matt. 10.34=Luke 12.51).

'I came to set a man against his father, and a daughter against her mother, and a daughter-in-law against her mother-in-law' (Matt. 10.35; cf. Luke 12.52).

'Do not think that I came to abolish the law and the prophets; I came not to abolish them but to fulfil them' (Matt. 5.17).

'I came not to call the righteous but sinners' (Mark 2.17 and pars.).

'The Son of man came eating and drinking' (Matt. 11.19=Luke 7.34).

'The Son of man also came not to be served but to serve, and to give his life as a ransom for many' (Mark 10.45 and par.).

'The Son of man came to seek and to save the lost' (Luke 19.10; cf. 9.56, if part of the true text).

And with these may be coupled such words as:

'Let us go on to the next towns, that I may preach there also; for that is why I came out' (Mark 1.38; cf. Luke 4.43),

and

'Have you come to destroy us? I know who you are, the Holy one of God' (Mark 1.24 and par.; cf. Matt. 8.29).

These well-known sayings must be set out lest our treatment of the 'coming' of Jesus or the Son of man should become unbalanced. Important as the references are to a coming that has yet to take place, these—to a coming that has already begun—

are far more numerous, and, incidentally, far better attested.[1]

These sayings fit very well with the understanding of Jesus' ministry derived from those which mark its close. The whole ministry is a 'coming', fraught with theological significance, from the moment that he comes into Galilee to the final entry into Jerusalem. All Jesus' work may be comprehended as 'the coming of the Son of man' to 'this generation', the generation upon whom the long-awaited blessing and judgement of God at last has fallen. These are the days which prophets and righteous men longed to see (Matt. 13.16 f. = Luke 10.23 f.), in proportion as they are the days in which their blood is to be required (Matt. 23.35 f. = Luke 11.50 f.).

In this context, then, let us now consider the remaining sayings of Jesus which refer to a 'coming' of the Son of man (excepting, of course, those which speak of his coming in glory on the clouds, with which we have already dealt).

First, we may take a group of parables, since their connexion with that of the Wicked Husbandmen will form a convenient link. Indeed, this connexion is, I believe, no accident and provides the clue to their interpretation.

We may compare the opening of these four stories:

Mark 12.1	*Mark 13.34*	*Matt. 25.14 f.*	*Luke 19.12 f.*
'A man planted a vineyard, and set a hedge round it, and dug a pit for the winepress, and built a tower, and let it out to tenants, and went to another country.'	'It is like a man going on a journey, when he leaves home and puts his servants in charge, each with his own work.'	'For it is as when a man going on a journey called his servants and entrusted to them his property; to one he gave five talents, etc. . . . Then he went away.'	'A nobleman went into a far country to receive kingly power and then return. Calling ten of his servants, he gave them ten pounds, and said to them, "Trade with these till I come".'

[1] They are more or less evenly distributed between the four main Synoptic sources: 'Q', Mark, special Luke and special Matthew.

Alongside these may be set also the parable of Luke 13.6–9:

'A man had a fig tree planted in his vineyard; and he came seeking fruit on it and found none. And he said to the vinedresser, "Lo, these three years I have come seeking fruit on this fig tree, and I find none. Cut it down; why should it use up the ground?" And he answered him, "Let it alone, sir, this year also, till I dig about it and put on manure. And if it bears fruit next year, well and good; but if not, you can cut it down." '

There is an obvious similarity between this parable and the incident in Mark 11.13 f., where Jesus saw a fig-tree and coming to it found nothing on it but leaves. The setting of this incident in the tradition, in close proximity with the parable of the Wicked Husbandmen, suggests that it also may originally have been a parable. If so, then the fact that Jesus is said to approach the fig-tree 'from afar' may conceivably betray the fact that it once had an opening like the others.

Now there can be no doubt that in the first of these stories the vineyard is intended to stand for Israel. 'For', as Isaiah said in the parable on which it is modelled, 'the vineyard of the Lord of hosts is the house of Israel . . .; and he looked for justice, but behold, bloodshed' (Isa. 5.1–7). The allusion is unambiguous, and the reference of Jesus' story must be to the preceding history of the nation. God is conceived in the Old Testament period as an absentee landlord, and the rulers of Israel are his tenants. In Jesus he pays his final visit to the people of his holding.

This is the inevitable interpretation also of 'the fig tree planted in the vineyard', again a recognized symbol for Israel. The allusion is once more to the same context in Jeremiah:

'When I would gather them, says the Lord, there are no grapes on the vine, nor figs on the fig-tree; even the leaves are withered, and what I gave them has passed away from them' (8.13).

The reference of the words 'I have come seeking fruit' must, as in the parallel incident in Mark, be to the culminating crisis of the ministry of Jesus, who at his coming finds the nation barren and unprepared.

J.C.—E

Yet, in the other stories, the man going away for a long time is taken to refer, not to the forbearance of God in the history of his people, but to the absence of Jesus after the Resurrection; and his coming corresponds no longer to the present crisis of Jesus' ministry, but to his future return. The distant journey, isolated by our comparison, is not, to be sure, the point of any of these parables, and it becomes important only when they are applied to the delay of the *Parousia*.[1] It is simply a necessary part of the dramatic machinery,[2] and it would be a mistake to read any significance into it, no departure being mentioned in the parable of the Fig-tree at all.[3] The real question is whether the 'coming' in these other stories was originally intended to have the very different reference which the Evangelists have given to it.

It is inherently far more probable that those who first heard them were not intended to make this radical shift of key, but to see in them, as naturally they would, the same warning as in the stories of the Vineyard and the Fig-tree. On this showing, the parables were spoken, not to a future situation which had not even begun—to alert the Church for its Lord's return—but to the present crisis of the nation, when after so long a period of delegated responsibility its leaders were being faced with the use they had made of the privileges and opportunities God had accorded to them.

The process by which these parables were given a fresh application in the Christian tradition, from the history of Israel culminating in the ministry of Jesus to the history of the Church culminating in the Second Coming, has been traced

---

[1]As, probably, in the additions of Luke 19.11 ('because they supposed that the kingdom of God was to appear immediately') and Matt. 25.19 ('after a long time'; cf. 25.5). But Luke adds the point that the owner of the vineyard went away 'for a long time' (20.9), even though he does not apply the parable to the *Parousia*.

[2]Cf. Dodd, op. cit., p. 159.

[3]In the similar parables of watching, discussed below, there is also no such introduction, except in Mark 13.34-6, and there it probably belonged originally to another story. In that of the Thief it would be wholly inappropriate to suggest that he *returned*!

in detail by Dr Dodd in his *Parables of the Kingdom* (pp. 146–53) and more recently by Professor Jeremias in his *Parables of Jesus* (pp. 47–51). The case does not need to be stated again. But by way of illustration, we may take one passage, where my analysis would not exactly correspond with either of theirs.

In Luke 19 we have a parable which needs to be extracted and examined in its own right, because it appears in the tradition to have become fused and absorbed into another. It is difficult now to disentangle the two, for both evidently followed the same familiar pattern—departure, home-coming, reckoning—and all the stages in each story are no longer represented. There would seem, however, to be two distinct situations involved. The one story describes a master who commissions his slaves to do business in his absence. On his return he rewards them with property and punishment according to what they have made of their deposits (vv. 13, 15b–26). That is the familiar parable of the Pounds, with its parallel in the Matthean parable of the Talents (Matt. 25. 14–30).

The other story is this:

'A man of noble birth travelled to a far country to acquire for himself kingly power, and then come back. But his citizens hated him, and sent an embassy after him, saying: "We do not want this man to reign over us". And when he returned, having aquired the right to be king, . . .[1] he said: "But those enemies of mine who did not want me to reign over them, bring them here and slaughter them before me" ' (vv. 12, 14–15a, 27).

This story—the parable of the Prince Royal—may well have its origin, as has often been suggested,[2] in an actual

[1]The sequel is now lost in the reckoning of the other parable but is probably reflected in the fact that the slaves are rewarded, somewhat inappropriately, with 'cities' (contrast Matthew).

[2]Cf. T. W. Manson, *The Sayings of Jesus*, pp. 313–7; Jeremias, op. cit., p. 48; C. W. F. Smith, *The Jesus of the Parables*, p. 201. The last, who reaches very similar conclusions about the original application of the *Parousia* parables, also isolates this as a separate story from that of the Pounds, but regards it as an insertion of the Church.

incident of recent history recorded by Josephus (*Bell. Jud.* ii, 80; *Antt.* xvii, 299 f.), when Archelaus, on the death of his father, Herod the Great, visited Rome to get his kingship over Judaea confirmed, followed by a Jewish deputation commissioned to resist his appointment. But whether based on fact or fiction it has an obvious and immediate relevance to the Kingdom of God and to the present situation of the Jews. They too are faced with a man who claims to come from higher authority with the right to their allegiance: will they accept the rule which he brings, or will they reject him with the same disastrous consequences?

The meaning lies close at hand, as the Jewish leaders recognized well enough in the story of the Wicked Husbandmen. There is no need to transpose everything into the future to find its application. Indeed, in parabolic form for 'those without', we have here precisely the same teaching as Jesus gives to his disciples in Luke 22.29 f. There he tells them how he has come with the right to reign that God has made over to him. And, as his Father has delegated kingly power[1] to him, so he in turn gives places of authority within the Kingdom to his faithful—'to sit on thrones judging the twelve tribes of Israel'.[2] Whether this element of reward for the faithful was originally represented in the story of the Prince Royal, as in that of the Pounds, we cannot now be sure. In any case, in all these stories it is upon the fate of the *unfaithful* that the emphasis falls: for they are parables of *warning* to the Jewish people against their now all but inevitable fate.

While these parables close upon the threat of dispossession, that of Mark 13.33–7, which starts in the same way with a man going abroad, ends with the call to watchfulness. It is possible, as Professor Jeremias says (op cit., pp. 43 f.), that we have here another instance of two stories fused into one.

---

[1]βασιλείαν absolutely, exactly as in Luke 19.12 above.
[2]Cf. the echo of this in Rev. 3.20 f., 'He who conquers, I will grant him to sit with me on my throne, as I myself conquered and sat down with my Father on his throne', where, as in Luke 22.29 f., this theme is also combined with that of eating with Christ.

The opening of the parable of the Money in Trust, or one like it, may have become attached to that of the Householder returning late at night, to be found in Luke 12.35–40. For men tell their servants to wait up for them, not when they go abroad, but when they have been out to a party. In any case, it forms the natural link with the warnings to watchfulness contained in the three stories of Luke 12—those of the House-holder returning from the wedding (vv. 35–8), the Burglar (vv. 39 f. = Matt. 24.43 f.), and the Servant left in charge (vv. 41–6 = Matt. 24.45–51)—and with the parable of the Ten Virgins in Matt. 25.1–13 (cf. Luke 12.35 f.; 13.25).

All of these describe an unexpected coming which will lay bare the difference between those who are vigilant and careful for their responsibilities and those who are not. By the Evangelists, again, the parables are applied, quite naturally, to the period in which they lived—to the post-resurrection Church and to the return of Jesus at the *Parousia*. But is this their original setting? Once more, it would be otiose to repeat the careful investigation undertaken by others.[1] Details of exegesis may be questioned, but from the con-clusion of the matter as Professor Jeremias states it I would find it impossible to dissent: 'The . . . *Parousia*-parables which we have discussed', he says, 'were originally a group of crisis-parables. They were intended to arouse a deluded people and their leaders to a realization of the awful gravity of the moment. The catastrophe will come as unexpectedly as the nocturnal housebreaker, as the bridegroom arriving at mid-night, the master of the house returning late from the wedding-feast. . . . See that you be not taken unawares!' (op. cit., p. 52).

They were addressed, that is to say, not to the coming Church, but to the contemporaries of Jesus, warning them that the present situation in which they stood was one of impending and overwhelming crisis. Their generation was about to be overtaken by events that must finally decide their destiny as the People of God. As the ministry of Jesus reached its climax in the crowning act which God was bring-

[1] *Vide* Dodd, op. cit., pp. 154–74; Jeremias, op. cit., pp. 38–47.

ing to completion through it, in that messianic event for
which their entire history had been meant, the hour of their
visitation was at hand. Would they see it and respond in time?
Would Israel act like the faithful steward, conscious of her
immense endowments, and wise[1] to the crisis in which she
stood; or was her fate to be cut to pieces and her place to be
with the unfaithful?

This warning to watchfulness, to read the signs of the times
before it was too late, is reinforced at the close of the same
chapter, in Luke 12.54–13.9, by a string of further parables.
Everything, says Jesus, cries out to the Jews to use their
judgement and common sense. There is the lesson of nature,
the obvious signs of the weather; there is the lesson of human
conduct, of what a sensible man does when threatened with a
disastrous law-suit; there is the lesson of recent history, the
warning of those who perished under the cruelties of Pilate
or the tower of Siloam; and, finally, there comes the story we
have already considered of the fruitless fig-tree and of what
happens to that.

Of these parables the application cannot be in doubt; they
refer, and must refer, to the coming crisis, religious and political, precipitated by the rejection of Jesus and his message.
And this is not simply a crisis such as might overtake any
nation; it represents the end of the purpose of God with his
people—all that is meant by saying that in this event is to be
seen also the visitation of the Son of man and the judgement
of history in the kingdom of God.

There seems no particular reason why these parables also

[1]The parables both of the faithful steward (Luke 12.42–8) and
of the dishonest steward (Luke 16.1–13) make the same point. In
each case the man is commended because he is φρόνιμος, the virtue
also of the five wise virgins. It is this precious quality, of having a
sense of the eschatological situation, which Jesus requires of his
followers. The command to be 'wise as serpents and harmless as
doves', which has become absorbed, like so much else, into the
Matthean mission charge (Matt. 10.16), could well belong to this
same context: 'Be fully aware of the hour in which you stand; yet
do nothing to provoke it by violence!'

should not have been turned into warnings of the imminence of the *Parousia*. In fact others very like them have. Thus, in Mark 13.28 f., there is the other parable of the Fig-tree:

'From the fig-tree learn its lesson: as soon as its branch becomes tender and puts forth leaves, you know that summer is near. So also, when you see these things taking place, know that he is near, at the very gates.'

The application (which in the Markan context refers to the return of Christ at the end of the world) may, as so often with the parables, represent the commentary of the Evangelist. Yet if Jesus did point his own moral, there is every reason to suppose it to have been that of the other lessons from nature, namely, that what was upon his hearers, and now at their very gates, was the visitation of their nation and city which was coming as certainly and as suddenly as summer follows spring. For hardly has the fig-tree budded and broken into leaf than the fruit is upon it.[1]

Again, corresponding closely to the preceding parables of the Cloud and the South Wind, there is that of the Lightning in Luke 17.24:

'As the lightning flashes and lights up the sky from one side to the other, so will the Son of man be in his day.'

Here a double shift seems to have taken place. Not only has the image been applied to the *Parousia*, but the suddenness of the flash (cf. Luke 10.18), the fact that it lights up the whole sky *instantaneously*, is ceasing to be the point of comparison. This development is still more evident in the Matthean version (24.27):

'As the lightning comes from the east and shines as far as the west, so will be the coming of the Son of man.'

[1]For the stages of a tree's growth as a symbol, not, as for us, of gradualness, but of suddenness, cf. I Clem. XXIII.3–5; 'Ye fools, compare yourselves unto a tree; take a vine. First it sheddeth its leaves, then a shoot cometh, then a leaf, then a flower, and after these a sour berry, then a full ripe grape. Ye see that in a little time the fruit of the tree attaineth unto mellowness. Of a truth quickly and suddenly shall his will be accomplished (ταχὺ καὶ ἐξαίφνης τελειωθήσεται).'

The *Parousia*, that is to say, when it arrives is going to be universally visible; there will be no need to say, 'Look, here!' or 'Look, there it is!'.

These last exclamations, 'Lo! here! . . . Lo! there!', from their multiple attestation in the tradition (Mark 13.21 and par.; Luke 17.21; Luke 17.23 = Matt. 24.26), probably spring from a genuine saying of Jesus. But it is very questionable whether they originally had this application. They are most strikingly represented in the saying of Luke 17.20 f.:

'The kingdom of God is not coming with signs to be observed; nor will they say "Lo, here it is!" or "There!", for behold, the kingdom of God is in the midst of you.'

If, as Luke says, this is addressed to the Pharisees, it is difficult to see how it can naturally mean that the Kingdom is a spiritual possession within them. Nor, I believe, is it simply a reference to the realized eschatology of Jesus' presence in their midst. It is most simply taken in line with the other sayings in the context. The Kingdom of God, or the visitation of the Son of man, is coming upon his hearers not with the kind of process that will allow of leisurely or curious calculation, but in a flash. Suddenly it will be in their midst and they will not be prepared. In the words of Professor T. W. Manson, 'One moment the world is just its normal self: then Lo! the Kingdom of God is among you'.[1]

This comment in fact sums up very exactly the drift of the whole section which the saying introduces in the second half of Luke 17. This consists of more teaching on the same theme, warning against surprise by sudden disaster. But this time it is non-parabolic. Whereas the parables were addressed to 'those without', this is instruction for Jesus' own associates. It will, therefore, provide a useful check upon the conclusions derived from the parables.

It may well be said that, though in his address to the Jews

[1]Op. cit., p. 304, cf., among other advocates of this interpretation, R. Bultmann, *Theology of the New Testament*, I, p. 6.

Jesus would naturally be speaking to the crisis at present upon them, it is in the teaching given to the disciples, the nucleus of the coming Church, that we should expect the promise and the warning of his future advent. While it may be admitted, as Professor Jeremias has emphasized, that much of what was in the first instance spoken to Jesus' opponents was later reapplied to the hope of the Church, may there not also have been instruction which was *originally* given to the disciples to alert them to the *Parousia*, and to which later they assimilated the other sayings of the same kind, whose primary application would by then be outdated?

Of this, very reasonable, presumption the eschatological discourse in Luke 17.22–37 will serve as a good test, a better test indeed than the comparable discourse of Mark 13, where we have already had reason to conclude that the reference to the *Parousia* was not part of Jesus' own words. If we bracket material which appears to have been introduced from other strands of the tradition and now interrupts its connexion,[1] the passage reads as follows:

'And he said to the disciples, "The days are coming when you will desire to see one of the days of the Son of man, and you will not see it. . . . As it was in the days of Noah, so is it going to be in the days of the Son of man. They ate, they drank, they married, they were

[1]Vv. 23 f. (already discussed) is Q material on the same theme as 20 f.: 'And they will say to you, "Lo, there!" or "Lo, here!"'. Do not go, do not follow them. For as the lightning flashes and lights up the sky from one side to the other, so will the Son of man be in his day'. Being referred to the Son of man rather than to the Kingdom of God, it has been introduced by Luke after the reference to the Son of man in v. 22. V.25, 'But first he must suffer many things and be rejected by this generation', appears to be a Lucan editorial connexion, based on the Markan tradition (it is the only verse in the Gospels explicitly to link the suffering and the apocalyptic references to the Son of man). V.33, 'Whoever seeks to gain his life will lose it, but whoever loses his life will preserve it', is a floating saying, found also in Mark 8.35 and pars.; Matt. 10.39; and John 12.25. V.36 is probably to be rejected on textual grounds, as an assimilation from Matthew, but it makes no difference.

given in marriage, until the day when Noah entered the ark, and the flood came and destroyed them all. Likewise as it was in the days of Lot—they ate, they drank, they bought, they sold, they planted, they built, but on the day when Lot went out from Sodom fire and brimstone rained from heaven and destroyed them all—so will it be on the day when the Son of man is revealed. On that day, let him who is on the housetop, with his goods in the house, not come down to take them away; and likewise let him who is in the field not turn back. Remember Lot's wife. . . . I tell you, in that night there will be two men in one bed; one will be taken and the other left. There will be two women grinding together; one will be taken and the other left." And they said to him, "Where, Lord?" He said to them, "Where the body is, there the eagles will be gathered together".'

In Luke, as in Matt. 24.37–41, this teaching is throughout applied to the *Parousia*. As the passage stands, this reference is internally inconsistent. For injunctions to hasty evacuation, however swift, are obviously futile in connexion with a *Parousia* which is to come over the entire world like a flash of lightning. But may it not still have had reference to the *Parousia* before the parable of the lightning was assimilated to it?

In an excellent discussion of this very difficult passage Dr Glasson has pointed out (op. cit., pp. 83–8) that we have in it three parallel situations, of a period of 'days' followed in each case by a decisive 'day', which brings the period to a close. There are the days of Noah, ended by the day in which Noah entered the ark; the days of Lot, terminated by the day Lot went out from Sodom; and now the days of the Son of man, to reach their conclusion in the day when the Son of man is 'revealed'. The preliminary period in each case is one of normal life, when things go on in their usual carefree way. And so it is that men are going to look back on the present period—the days when the Son of man is with them— and wish that they could have them again.[1] But, as in the two

---

[1]This verse, 'The days are coming when you will desire to see one of the days of the Son of man, and you will not see it', is regularly regarded as clear piece of evidence that Jesus contemplated an

previous instances, the days of apparent calm are but the prelude to a moment which must mark a final break with the existing careless order. Those who survive that day will be those who, like Noah and Lot, are prepared to take decisive action and come out, with not so much as a backward glance at the old order. For remember Lot's wife.

In the present situation too the decisive action demanded will be immediate flight from a doomed city. If you should be on the roof, down you must slip by the outer stairs and not even go in for your things; if you are in the fields, you must go straight from there without turning back, even (as the parallel tradition in Mark says) to pick up your coat. This other tradition, in Mark 13.14–20, puts beyond doubt that the reference is to the fall of Jerusalem, the external climax to that judgement upon the nation which even now is being written. When it comes it will come like the Flood; and, as in Noah's time, the ones 'left' (not, that is to say, those abandoned but those spared)[1] will be men alert enough to see what is coming and flee to the hills. The rest will be 'taken', with the city and all that is in it.

It is possible that the enigmatic words with which the passage ends may also point to Jerusalem as the scene of destruction.

'They said to him, "Where, Lord?" He said to them, "Where the body is, there the eagles will be gathered together".'

Matthew has this, without the introductory question, in conjunction with the saying about the flash of lightning; and it may well be another little parable of the imminent catastrophe: 'Where the carcass is, there, in an instant [cf. Job 9.25 f.;

---

interval between his death and *parousia* (e.g., C. J. Cadoux, op. cit., p. 303; Kümmel, op. cit., pp. 29, 79). If, as I am convinced, the correct interpretation is that given above, then one of the chief arguments for this supposition falls to the ground.

[1] Cf. Gen. 7.23: 'Only Noah was left, and those that were with him in the ark'.

Hab. 1.8] will the vultures be'. But if Luke's placing is right, there may possibly be a veiled reference to the account of the desolation of the City and Temple in Jeremiah 7. It was a chapter upon which Jesus had evidently meditated deeply, with its message that 'This is the nation that did not obey the voice of the Lord their God' and that therefore 'the Lord has rejected and forsaken the generation of his wrath' (vv. 28 f.). From it he had taken his description of the Temple as 'a den of robbers' (v. 11) and his allusion to God 'sending the prophets, day after day' without result (vv. 25 f.). Finally, it concludes, when 'the land becomes a waste', 'the dead bodies of this people will be food for the birds of the air' (vv. 33 f.; cf. 34.20). So here too Jesus' reply to the question, 'Where, Lord?', may contain a cryptic allusion to Jerusalem as the city of doom.

As Dr Glasson, who makes this suggestion, goes on to say, this teaching was evidently not lost upon the disciples. When the time came, the Christians in Jerusalem made good their escape to Pella. Indeed, one might even hazard the suggestion that the 'oracle' to which the Church historian Eusebius refers in this connexion (*Hist. Eccl.* III, 5, 3), as 'given out by revelation' may actually still be preserved (as 'a word of the Lord') in the Jerusalem source of Matt. 10.23; namely: 'If they persecute you in this city [i.e., Jerusalem] flee to the other[1] [i.e. by pre-arrangement, Pella]'.

But, in any case, the relevant point here is that what is applied by the Evangelists to the *Parousia* has been found once more to have its reference to the imminent catastrophe which must spell the doom of the nation. In these sayings Jesus is again referring to the same crisis, spiritual and physical, of which the parables spoke. But here he is no longer warning the Jews to avert it, but preparing the dis-

---

[1]εἰς τὴν ἑτέραν. While this suggestion is entirely speculative, it seems to me more plausible than the identification of the oracle which has at various times been made with the whole of the so-called 'little apocalypse' of Mark 13 (cf. Beasley-Murray, op. cit., pp. 242–4).

ciples for their response to the inevitable. For, unless they
are alert to the judgements of God, they too will perish.

This approaching hour is that which is going to bring to a
close 'the days of the Son of man'. In this it is parallel to the
day when Noah entered the ark and Lot went out from Sodom.
What Jesus saw as the corresponding action of the Son of
man he does not specify. But as he persistently associates the
judgement of the City with his own rejection, there can be
little doubt that he knew it to be that departure which he too
must shortly accomplish at Jerusalem (Luke 9.31).[1]

All the lines meet, that is to say, in a point where the crisis
brought by his ministry comes to its head. This crisis will have
a number of aspects. Outwardly it will mean the destruction of
the nation. This, indeed, will not come at once. 'Do not weep
for me', says Jesus, 'but weep for yourselves and for your
children. . . . For if they do this when the wood is green,
what will happen when it is dry?' (Luke 23.28–31). The point
of combustion, physically speaking, has not been reached:
the disciples have still to be prepared for something lying
ahead and warned not to be caught napping. Yet spiritually
the hour of judgement comes with the moment of Jesus'
rejection. For then it is that the nation makes the great
refusal: thereafter the forces that will lead in the course of
history to the Jewish revolt are irrevocably set in motion.

But it is not merely in terms even of a spiritual decision
that Jesus views this moment, but in terms of an act of God;
or, rather, in terms of *the* act of God. For Jewish history is not
just ordinary history: it is the history of salvation, the story
of God's redemptive plan. And the event towards which it
moves cannot but be also the ultimate act of *God*, the messianic
event. That, for the chosen people, is its ineluctable destiny,
even if it should turn out to be its doom.

And so it is that Jesus uses of this event language entirely

[1]It is perhaps worth noting that in I Peter 3.18–22 the death and
resurrection of Christ, re-presented in the act of baptism, are compared with God's saving act in 'the days of Noah', and that in Rev.
11.8 the city where the Lord was crucified is called Sodom.

disproportionate to that which the purely historical situation would warrant. For, did the Jews but know it, in rejecting him they are rejecting God. The hour of their visitation is not simply the crisis of *any* nation: it is 'the day of the Son of man', that moment in which God's purpose for all history comes to final definition.

This language is clearly reflected in the passage we have been studying. And without doubt it is this language which has caused the Evangelists to apply Jesus' words, not to the historical situation to which originally they were tied, but to something outside history altogether. 'The day' which is to conclude 'the days of the Son of man' is turned into a purely supernatural event at the end of the world, in face of which it is entirely irrelevant whether a man goes home to collect his coat or not. This event is described by Matthew (24.39) as 'the *parousia* of the Son of man'—a term which is clearly editorial on its first appearance (24.3) and which evidently betrays the usage of the Church. Luke styles it 'the day on which the Son of man is *revealed*', a phrase which again almost certainly reflects not the words of Jesus—it is unique in the Gospels—but the technical term, 'the revelation of our Lord Jesus Christ', employed by the early Church.

It is therefore impossible to be certain how Jesus spoke of this moment before it became identified with the *Parousia*. All we can be sure of is that he associated it in some way with 'the Son of man', since the entire ministry which led up to it could be described as 'the days of the Son of man'.[1] Beyond that we cannot be sure; but Jesus may well have spoken of it in terms of the 'coming' of the Son of man. Otherwise, indeed, it is not easy to see how this phrase found its way into the

[1]One could argue by inference to the term 'the day of the Son of man' (and see in it the origin of 'the day of our Lord Jesus Christ' of the Epistles). But the phrase does not actually occur. The nearest approach is in Luke 17.24: 'So will the Son of man be in his day'. But even here some of the best authorities (B, D, 220, a, b, e, i, sa) omit 'in his day'. For 'so will be the Son of man' standing alone, cf. Luke 11.30: 'So will the Son of man be to this generation'.

tradition.[1] The actual evidence for this is, to be sure, very slender—and it is nothing like as well authenticated as the sayings which speak of the Son of man having come. It is preserved for us, in fact, in three isolated, and on critical grounds, rather dubious, sayings.

(1) The first is in the moral attached to the parable of the Burglar:

'You also must be ready; for the Son of man is coming at an hour you do not expect' (Luke 12.40 = Matt. 24.44).

Professor Jeremias has no hesitation in rejecting this as subsequent allegorization, whereby the figure of the parable becomes identified with Jesus himself.[2] Like all the other applications of parables it is highly suspect, and he is probably right. But it does represent the sole case of verbal agreement in such language between Matthew and Luke (unless, indeed, the text of Luke has here been assimilated to that of Matthew, as Harnack thought).[3] This in itself proves no more than that the application had already been made in their common source. But it is quite possible that Jesus did in some way describe the catastrophe for which the entry of the burglar stood, as a 'coming of the Son of man'.[4] For this crisis was

[1] It could, of course, be regarded as an extension and misunderstanding of the language about the coming of the Son of man on the clouds. But this language belongs wholly to the Markan tradition, whereas the coming of the Son of man in visitation is found exclusively in 'Q', special Matthew and special Luke. If it were a case of the coming of 'the Lord', we could look to the community tradition represented in the Epistles and derive it ultimately from the language of the LXX (*vide* below pp. 140 f.).

[2] Op. cit., pp. 39 f. A very similar instance of such allegorization is clearly to be seen in Matt. 24.42, 'Watch therefore, for you do not know on what day *your Lord* is coming', compared with the 'Watch, therefore, for you do not know when the master of the house will come' of Mark 13.35.

[3] *The Sayings of Jesus*, pp. 31, 34; cf. Glasson, op. cit., p. 95. Luke 12.40 is omitted by MSS. of fam. 1. It would not then have stood in 'Q', but be a Matthean editorial addition, like Matt. 24.42 and 25.13.

[4] It is surely no objection, as Jeremias suggests (op. cit., pp. 39 f.),

after all but the climax of that visitation in which his whole ministry consisted.

(2) The same conception may lie behind the equally dubious saying to be found in Matt. 10.23:

'If they persecute you in this city, flee to the next (*or* the other); for truly, I say to you, you will not have gone through all the cities of Israel, before the Son of man comes.'

In the context of the Mission of the Twelve in which Matthew places it this is in plain contradiction with the warning that the disciples will have to appear before Gentiles (Matt. 10.18). Like the whole section to which it is attached, which has been transferred here by Matthew from the Markan apocalypse (Matt. 10.17–22 = Mark 13.9–13), it is more easily fitted into a situation after the death of Jesus than into anything we know of the Ministry itself. It is probably best connected with the harrying Christians must expect when the country finally collapses. In what form, if any, it goes back to Jesus, we shall consider in the next chapter. But it *may* again provide some witness to his description of the nation's doom in terms of a 'coming' of the Son of man.

(3) Finally, in Luke 18.8, after the promise of imminent vindication appended to the parable of the Widow and the Judge,

'And will not God vindicate his elect who cry to him day and night? Will he delay long over them? I tell you he will vindicate them speedily,'

there is, as we saw, the further question:

'Nevertheless, when the Son of man comes, will he find faith on earth?'

Those critics are probably right who see here a subsequent

---

that this is 'a disastrous and alarming event'; for that is precisely what it would be to those to whom the parable was originally addressed.

addition,[1] reflecting the Church's apprehension for the faithfulness of Christians as the End approaches; for this is a
concern to be found elsewhere in the Lucan writings (Luke
21.34–6; Acts 20.28–31). But the possibility cannot be ex-
cluded that, if Jesus did here speak of such an imminent
vindication, he should have gone on to describe the same
moment also as a visitation of the Son of man, whose requirement would be faith. For was not this moment, more even
than the rest of the ministry which preceded it, to be seen as
the coming of the Son of man to find faith in Israel (cf. Luke
7.9)?

The evidence to support the conclusion that Jesus spoke of
the final crisis specifically as a 'coming of the Son of man' is
indeed slender compared with that for regarding his entire
ministry in terms of such a visitation. But what, I believe, is
clear is that there is in his teaching no 'coming of the Son of
man' which does *not* refer to this ministry, its climax and its
consequences. The visitation in judgement of which he spoke
would indeed merely be *set in motion* by his rejection. Its
outworking, like his own vindication, would take place 'from
now on'. As in glory, so in visitation, we must speak, not of a
realized, but of an inaugurated eschatology, of the Son of
man 'coming to his own' in all the power of God, till the
kingdoms of this world shall have become the kingdom of
God and of his Christ. For Jesus the messianic act would
certainly not be exhausted in his death and resurrection. On
the contrary, this moment would but release and initiate
that reign of God in which *henceforth* the Father's redeeming
work could be brought to the fulfilment which hitherto it was
denied.

But what fails is the evidence that Jesus thought of the
messianic act as taking place in two stages, the first of which
was now shortly to be accomplished, the second of which
would follow after an interval and must in the meantime be
the focus of every eye and thought. For we have now reviewed

[1] E.g., J. M. Creed, *St Luke*, ad loc.; Jeremias, op. cit., p. 84;
Kümmel, op. cit., p. 59 n. 126.

all the sayings about the coming of the Son of man, whether in vindication or in visitation. And in them we have found nothing requiring us to suppose that Jesus envisaged a second such moment of the Son of man, beyond and separate from the culmination of the ministry which he came to fulfil.[1] We are far from saying that he could not have done so—merely that the evidence fails that he did. In all the decisive cases his words have a more natural application, not to a future advent, but to those climactic events in which he himself stood; though it is equally natural that the Church, which did not stand in these events, should later have adapted the teaching to its own hope.

This does not mean that we have now finished with the evidence of the Gospels. Indeed, our problems have really only begun. And the heart of the problem is this: If what we have said is true, how did it come about that Jesus was understood, and represented by the Evangelists, so differently? For if the Church's *Parousia* hope does not go back to Jesus, from where does it come? We are no nearer the answer to that question. All we have done so far is to deprive ourselves of what is on all counts the simplest explanation.

[1]So Dodd, op. cit., p. 154; Duncan, op. cit., pp. 182–9.

4

FROM THE EXPECTATION OF JESUS TO
THAT OF THE CHURCH

THAT the heart of the Christian hope was now, once more, to 'wait for God's Son from heaven', for a second and final coming which would complete and crown the first, is a belief for which we have found no firm foundation in the words of Jesus himself. In consequence we are left with a gulf fixed. There appears to be no way across from the teaching of Jesus, as we leave it about the year 30, to the expectation of the Church, as we find Paul preaching it in Thessalonica about the year 50. Yet nothing is more certain than that the transition was made.

How and why was it made? Without an answer to these questions doubt must be thrown on the adequacy of our analysis—and particularly upon our conclusion that Jesus himself looked for no such event as the Church expected. For the Gospels as they stand do represent him as doing so. The burden of proof rests upon those who would deny that these sayings represent the mind of Jesus. That burden can be shifted only by a sufficient explanation, first, of *how* Jesus came to be understood by the Church to predict his return, and, secondly, of *why* this expectation arose, if in fact it was not derived from him. In this and the two following chapters therefore we shall examine the actual process of transition, first from Jesus to the Church, and then within the thinking of the Church itself. After that we must try to probe to the underlying causes: *Why* did the Church come to entertain the unprecedented notion of a second coming at all?

We may begin with some sayings which have always lain at

the heart of the belief that Jesus expected a second imminent event within the life-time of his contemporaries—sayings like those of Mark 9.1, 'There are some standing here who will not taste death before they see the kingdom of God come with power', and Mark 13.30, 'This generation will not pass away before all these things take place'. There is no actual mention here of a *Parousia*, and for this reason we have not yet had occasion to consider them. But in the Gospel tradition they are closely associated with this expectation. Thus, in the former passage, Matthew, as we have seen, substitutes the words, 'Before they see the Son of man coming in his king-dom' (16.28); and, in the Markan apocalypse, 'all these things' are clearly intended to include the coming of the Son of man on the clouds described a few verses earlier (13.26). What, then, are we to make of these sayings, which do appear to speak of a second and imminent event, linked, at any rate by the Evangelists, with the coming of the Son of man?

We shall later have occasion to scrutinize the link which the Evangelists have here made; but for the moment let us accept that there is behind the sayings an original connexion of some kind between 'the coming of the Son of man' and 'this generation'. For this association, in one form or other, is widely attested in the Gospels. It is interesting to observe that it cuts right across the traditional division of the Son of man sayings (into those that seem simply to mean 'I' or 'man', those of humiliation, and those of glory). It also cuts across the different strands of the Gospel material, which suggests that the juxtaposition is not purely editorial.

We may consider the following sayings:

'To what shall I compare this generation? . . . For John came neither eating nor drinking, and they say, "He has a demon"; the Son of man came eating and drinking, and they say, "Behold, a glutton and a drunkard, a friend of tax collectors and sinners!" ' (Matt. 11.16–19 = Luke 7.31–4).

'As Jonah was a sign to the men of Nineveh, so will the Son of man be to this generation' (Luke 11.30).[1]

---

[1]In Matt. 12.39 f., the connexion is weakened. The original

'Whoever is ashamed of me and of mine in this adulterous and sinful generation, of him will the Son of man also be ashamed, when he comes in the glory of his Father' (Mark 8.38).

'So will the Son of man be in his day. But first he must suffer many things and be rejected of this generation' (Luke 17.24 f.).

All these in some way relate the coming of the Son of man to the crisis of the present generation, a coming which the very title 'the Son of man' indicates to be ultimate and decisive in its significance. It is those among whom Jesus is moving and teaching and by whom he is being rejected who are face to face with the End. The very presence of the Son of man in its midst is to prove to this generation the sign that Jonah was to the Ninevites—the final warning that it must repent or perish. Even where the connexion must be ascribed to the Evangelists,[1] the reference of 'this generation' is still to the present period of the Ministry itself.

This teaching is merely summed up in the saying we have examined earlier, that 'the blood of all the prophets, shed from the foundation of the world' is to 'be required of this generation' (Luke 11.50 f.).

It is at this point, however, that we may watch the transformation beginning. In the Lucan and more original version of this saying, it is the blood of Israel's past which is to be required of this generation. In Matthew (23.34–6), Jesus is made to speak of the treatment that is still to be accorded to the Christian mission and of the judgement that must follow, and he ends: 'Truly, I say to you, all this will come upon this generation'. The phrase has started to become a *terminus ad*

---

point (Matt. 12.41 = Luke 11.32), that the preaching of Jonah was to his generation what the preaching of the Son of man is to this, is overlaid by Jonah's escape from the whale being treated as a type of the Resurrection.

[1]This we have argued (p. 73) to be the case in Luke 17.24 f. In Mark 8.38 it is only the coming in glory that may be secondary: the association of the Son of man with the saying is attested by the parallel in 'Q' (Luke 12.8).

quem, a time limit within which certain future events will occur. And this process is simply completed in Mark 13.30: 'Truly, I say to you, this generation will not pass away, before all these things take place'. Here it has a purely chronological significance, fixing the extreme limit of a carefully graduated apocalyptic programme.

How purely temporal the phrase has become is borne out by the way in which two verses later, in Mark 13.32, the saying about 'that day or that hour' has been incorporated into the same time-table. As the passage now stands, the generation, the span of years, within which all will occur is declared to be certain, and can be disclosed; but the precise moment within it, the day and the hour, is known only to God—though it *is* known to him.

But in this second saying there would appear to be a further instance of Jesus' words being revalued in a purely chronological sense. For this interpretation, with the implication, unparalleled in his teaching, that God works to a pre-determined schedule, rests entirely upon the assumption that the two sayings belong together and that the express purpose of the second is to qualify the first. Since, however, the final verses of Mark 13 appear to be a collection of isolated sayings, with parallels in widely diverse parts of the Gospel tradition,[1] this is a most precarious assumption. By itself, and with no prior allusion to 'this generation', the phrase 'that day' or 'that hour'[2] would naturally refer, as it regularly does (e.g. Matt. 7.22; Luke 10.12), to the one Day which required no further specification, and which was by its very nature 'known (only) to the Lord' (Zech. 14.7; cf. II Baruch 21.8), because it was his alone to dispose (Acts 1.7). That Jesus spoke, like every Jew, of this final 'day of the Lord', when all would be

[1] With vv. 28 f. cf. Luke 12.54–6; v. 30 cf. Matt. 23.36; v. 31 cf. Matt. 5.18 = Luke 16.17; vv. 33–34a cf. Matt. 25.13 f.; vv. 34b–36 cf. Luke 12.36–8.

[2] The two are most naturally taken as parallel expressions. Cf. the alternation between 'the last day' and 'the last hour' in John 5.28; 6.39–54; 11.24; 12.48; I John 2.18; and the similar parallelism between 'the times' and 'the seasons' in Acts 1.7.

brought to an end, we have already seen.[1] In view of the peculiar relation to it which he claimed for himself (Matt. 7.22 f.; 10.32 f.; Luke 12.8 f.; 13.25–7), we can well understand that he should have found it necessary to dissociate himself, even as 'the Son', from the knowledge of its hour. Moreover, the eschatological language in which he sought to interpret the 'consummation' of his own life and ministry as Son of man must have made it the more imperative for him to distinguish this consummation from the final 'day of God'. For there is no compelling reason to believe that he equated the two, no real indication that he thought that the end of his life would also mark the end of history: indeed, there is the strongest evidence to suggest that he envisaged a situation where the disciples would be left to carry on in the world without him.

But if this was the original reference of the saying—to an 'hour' and a 'day' which was not to be defined chronologically at all, but in terms of the *kairos* or goal to which all history moves—its juxtaposition with the words about 'this generation' has drawn it into the same process of revaluation to which they have been subjected, and of which we shall be seeing other examples.

Indeed, between these two verses (and associating the passing of this generation with the end of the world) Mark places the words: 'Heaven and earth will pass away, but my words will not pass away'; and it is interesting to observe how a saying very similar to this has been submitted to precisely the same process. In Luke 16.17 occur the words: 'It is easier for heaven and earth to pass away, than for one dot of the law to become void'. In Matt. 5.18 this simple comparison is given a temporal twist, by the addition of a phrase which appears to betray the direct influence of the connexion made in Mark 13.30 f.: 'Till heaven and earth pass away, not an iota, not a dot, will pass from the law *until all is accomplished*'. The sense here is unchanged;[2] but it illustrates a process at work

[1] p. 37 above.
[2] Though cf. T. W. Manson, op. cit., p. 135.

which in the sayings about 'this generation' makes a very real difference.

We must try to define this difference more closely, as it is important for understanding what happened in the early Church to much of the teaching of Jesus.

On the one hand, one can make statements like, 'Now is the day of salvation', 'This is the generation upon which the hour of decision has come'. Such judgements are concerned with the decisive character of the moment of which they speak, not with its duration in terms of hours or years. To say, 'This was their finest hour', is to specify nothing about the length of the crisis. And when Jesus pronounced that the blood of all the prophets was to be required of that generation, he was not predicting how long it would be before the reckoning was over.

But, with very little alteration, any of these statements can be given a chronological rather than a moral significance. 'This is the day!' can be presented in the form: 'This day, or this generation, will not have passed before the decisive thing happens'. Then the focus of attention is subtly shifted, and whether the twenty-four hours is up or the requisite number of years has elapsed makes all the difference. In the first case, the mere passage of time cannot affect the truth of the judgement; in the second, if the day or generation goes by and nothing happens, the statement is discredited. Moreover, to say, 'This is the generation upon which all has come', is to concentrate everything upon the decisiveness of the present moment; to say, 'This generation will not pass away until . . .', is to focus attention, not on the present, but upon whatever it is that has still to occur.

It is this shift of emphasis which, I believe, may be seen at work upon the sayings of Jesus and was to prove one of the most potent factors in attributing to him a concern with a second event lying beyond his own ministry. In the course of transmission his teaching became focused not upon the present event whose urgency he was proclaiming but upon another event whose imminence he was predicting. And words that he spoke of the one came in the tradition to be applied to the other. 'This generation', from designating, in terms of the moral crisis, the moment during which the End and its judgement are set within the present, comes to describe, in purely chronological terms, the span of time still left before the End, within which all must be fulfilled.

The process, once recognized, may also throw light on other passages where prediction is made of certain things that will or will not take place *before* the End.

Thus, there is the other saying mentioned at the beginning of the chapter, that of Mark 9.1:

'Truly, I say to you, there are some standing here who will not taste death before they see the kingdom of God come with power.'

Now Mark presumably (as Matthew explicitly) intends the moment here described to be identified with that of the Son of man's coming in glory, of which he has spoken in the previous verse (8.38). But if, as we argued,[1] this clause is not original to Jesus (or if it refers to an entry *into* his glory) it would be most natural, in the wider context of Mark 8.31–8, to understand the declaration of 9.1 as a prophecy of early vindication, similar to that before the Sanhedrin in 14.62, and describing the same event. Jesus would then be referring not to a second moment at an interval (of a generation or so) after his death, but, as in all the other sayings we have investigated, to that climax out of suffering which was about to come with his death and vindication to the right hand of God. Since, then, the saying is perfectly intelligible as it stands, this is perhaps the most satisfactory explanation.

But there is something to be said for thinking that originally it did not have a chronological reference at all, but related to the conditions, rather than to the date, of the Kingdom's coming. On this interpretation, the 'tasting of death' is not merely a more poetic way of saying 'within this generation', but conceals the clue to the meaning of the words.

The release of the Kingdom in power we have already seen

[1]pp. 53–6 above.

to have been closely associated by Jesus with his death. Moreover, what he thus described as the baptism he had to complete (Luke 12.50) he appears, at any rate at one stage, to have expected would be shared literally by his followers: 'The cup that I drink you will drink; and with the baptism with which I am baptized, you will be baptized' (Mark 10.39).[1] Indeed, immediately prior to the words we are considering he has been insisting that anyone who would follow him must be ready to take up his cross and lose his life (Mark 8.34 f.).[2] But at the same time he must have known that the mass of the people would never become disciples at this level.

Now the section in which all this occurs is addressed, uniquely in the Gospels, to 'the multitude with the disciples' (Mark 8.34).[3] The connexion of 9.1 with this introduction may, of course, be purely editorial; but it does explain its rather curious phrasing, which runs literally, according to what is probably the best text: 'I say to *you* that there are some here of the bystanders'.[4] This does sound precisely as if Jesus is addressing the disciples in the presence of the crowds. May it be that having just sought to communicate to the disciples the necessary connexion of the Kingdom's coming with his death (vv. 31-3), and called any who would follow him to the same sacrifice (vv. 34-8), he then affirms that nevertheless many of those in the crowd (like the Sanhedrin later) will see the King-

---

[1] Cf. Schweitzer, *The Mystery of the Kingdom of God*, pp. 219-26.

[2] This whole passage is one of the most powerful supports for the thesis of T. W. Manson, recently restated in his contribution to *Studies in the Gospels* (ed. D. E. Nineham), pp. 215-22, that 'the Son of man' both in suffering and resurrection is by its very nature a corporate term.

[3] In the parallel in Matt. 16.24 it is, 'to the disciples'; and in Luke 9.23, 'to all'. The nearest equivalent to this situation is to be found in Luke 12.1.

[4] τινες ὧδε τῶν ἑστηκότων (B). This is adopted by Taylor, ad loc. Both Matthew and Luke have the more natural τινες τῶν ὧδε (αὐτοῦ) ἑστηκότων, reflected also in most of the other MSS. of Mark (P.45 has τῶν ἑστηκότων ὧδε). For οἱ ἑστηκότες as 'the bystanders', cf. Matt. 26.73; John 3.29; Acts 22.25.

dom come as an objective fact,[1] even though they will have had no share in the death through which alone its glory can break? If this was his meaning, it was clearly misunderstood; and it was this misunderstanding perhaps which lies behind the expectation, corrected in John 21.23, that some of *the disciples* would never die.

In its present shape the saying has a purely chronological reference, and, from the connexion with the previous verse, is evidently intended to apply to the *Parousia*.[2] But what has come to be a temporal prediction, which at the time of the Evangelist could still be fulfilled, may have begun rather as an assertion of the inner moral relation of the coming of the Kingdom with suffering and death. This cannot be demonstrated, and the saying, despite its present application, may still be preserved in its original form. But such a shift would be in line with the same transition we observed from a moral to a chronological connexion between the coming of the Son of man and the judgement of this generation.

It is possible too that the saying in Matt. 10.23,

'You will not have gone through all the towns of Israel, before the Son of man comes,'

[1] ἐληλυθυῖαν.

[2] It is possible, as G. Bornkamm has suggested ('Die Verzögerung der Parusie', *In Memoriam Ernst Lohmeyer* (ed. W. Schmauch), pp. 116–9), that its present form reflects the Church's reaction to the delay of the *Parousia*. By then it is recognized that *some* only of that generation will survive to see it (cf. I Thess. 4.13–18; I Cor. 15.51). O. Cullmann ('The Return of Christ', *The Early Church*, p. 152) draws the conclusion that 'Jesus seems to have envisaged the lapse of at least several decades before the arrival of the kingdom, since he says that "some" of his contemporaries would survive to see it'. But on the very next page he says: 'According to Jesus himself, his death is the decisive event which ushers in the coming of the kingdom'. To reconcile such remarks he invokes the idea of two moments in the divine drama separated by an interval, but has to admit that 'in the three statements of Jesus we have studied [Mark 9.1; 13.30; Matt. 10.23], the first and the last divine decision are not distinguished' (ibid., p. 154). They are in fact merely read into the material.

may reflect the same process. We have already argued that these words are best associated with the reign of terror associated with the fall of Jerusalem. That Jesus foresaw some such situation is by no means improbable. 'If they do this when the wood is green, what will happen when it is dry?' (Luke 23.31): such is the logic that perceives in the grim realities of the Crucifixion but the 'beginning of the sufferings' that must overtake the nation (Mark 13.8). Indeed, as we have seen, the paragraph to which our present saying is added (Matt. 10. 17–22) is detached by Matthew from one of the many passages in which these sufferings are described (Mark 13. 9–20).[1] That this entire situation should have been interpreted by Jesus in terms of the visitation of the Son of man we have also seen reason to regard as probable. May it be that a saying giving this prophetic interpretation to the coming crisis has here again received a chronological twist, to provide the assurance that certain events will not have occurred *before* the Son of man comes? We cannot be sure. But it is interesting that each of these last three sayings has precisely the same structure, a strong negative asseveration followed by a temporal clause:

'Truly, I say to you, this generation will not pass away before all these things take place.'

'Truly, I say to you, there are some standing here who will not taste death before they see the kingdom of God come with power.'

'Truly, I say to you, you will not have gone through all the towns of Israel before the Son of man comes.'

In the first two cases there were grounds for thinking that their present temporal form might be secondary: it is at least possible that the third has undergone the same transformation.[2]

[1]Cf. Luke 12.11 f.; 19.41–4; 21.12–24; 23.28–31.

[2]It is not implied that all sayings in this shape are secondary (cf., e.g., Mark 14.25; Luke 22.16–18, the vow of abstinence at the Last Supper). But Matt. 23.39, 'I tell you, you will not see me again, until you say, "Blessed be he who comes in the name of the Lord" ', shows how naturally this form of promise could be adapted to the *Parousia* hope.

In all this, as in every reconstruction which attempts to go behind the Evangelists to Jesus, much must inevitably be speculative. It is, however, possible, I believe, to detect a fairly clear process of development by which the accent of finality comes to be lifted from the ministry of Jesus itself and its consequences and laid upon a second event expected after it, at whatever interval. To this event are transferred those warnings and promises in which Jesus sought originally to define the crisis that his presence involved. The really decisive 'coming of the Son of man' is projected into an imminent but ever receding future.

This is the process we detected at work upon the parables of crisis;[1] and it is most clearly illustrated in the transmission of another saying we have already had occasion to notice.[2]

The 'Q' tradition lying behind Matthew and Luke contains the words:

'Everyone who acknowledges me before men, the Son of man also will acknowledge before the angels of God, but he who denies me before men will be denied before the angels of God' (Luke 12.8 f.).

According to this, men are in the presence of the eschatological event. Their reaction to Jesus now is to have eternal consequences; for in him God's final word is being spoken, and 'the last day' will but reflect this day. The eschatology is given in, with and under the historical event: it is represented in the accent of finality placed upon the present claims and demands of Jesus.

But in the Markan version of the same saying there is, as we saw, the beginning of a further development:

'Whoever is ashamed of me and of mine in this adulterous and sinful generation of him will the Son of man also be ashamed, *when he comes in the glory of his Father with the holy angels*' (8.38).

The present is still the crucial moment, but there is also to be another eschatological event, a second 'coming', which has yet to take place.

[1] pp. 64–72. [2] pp. 53–6.

The process is completed by Matthew. In his parallel to this verse, the original saying, which stressed the decisive character of Jesus' present ministry, has disappeared altogether. The eschatology is represented solely by a future event, expanded from the Markan addition:

'The Son of man is to come with his angels in the glory of his Father, and then he will repay every man for what he has done' (16.27).

This statement is then in its turn written up by Matthew into a full-scale vision of the Last Assize, whose introduction, with its elaborate reference to the *Parousia,* is, I believe, demonstrably of his own composing:[1]

'When the Son of man comes in his glory, and all the angels with him, then he will sit on his glorious throne; and before him will be gathered all the nations . . .' (25.31 ff.).

This development may be described in another way by saying that the teaching of Jesus underwent the same sort of shift of key that occurred in the Old Testament in the transition from the eschatology of the Prophets to that of the Apocalyptic writers.

For the Prophets eschatology was a way of understanding history, the history in which they were living, *sub specie finis:* they looked out on the world scene and set it always in the light of the ultimate meaning and judgement of God. In order to express and clarify that meaning and judgement, as it came to them even now through the relativities of current events, they were driven to myths of the future in which the blacks and whites were no longer blurred and confused, as in the baffling contradictions of the present. But through such pictures of the Last Days their concern was always to bring to bear upon the *present* the promise and the warning contained in the end of the ways of God. They were concerned with the End, not for providing a map of the future, but for supplying a criterion for the present. For them eschatology was not a separate depart-

---

[1] *Vide* again my article in *N.T. Studies,* II (1956), pp. 226–9.

ment, dealing with the hereafter, with a subject-matter of its own; rather, it represented a perspective, a dimension of reality, in which the whole of life took on a new and radical seriousness. It did not treat only of the things that were going to happen after everything else; it treated of everything, in the light of the End. Indeed, one could not talk meaningfully of 'eschatology' in contradistinction to 'ethics': one could only have an eschatological ethic—one, like that of Amos, which reckoned with the ultimate, with the Day of the Lord—or a non-eschatological ethic.

But, with the Apocalyptists, eschatology developed into a subject in itself, a science of the End, a description—the more detailed the better—of what was going to happen hereafter, whether in history or beyond it. And one could produce treatises on the last things and treatises on ethics, the one dealing with the future, the other with the present. And for late Judaism the two were distinct, the apocalyptic writers giving schematic arrangement to the divine promises, the scribal tradition providing precise codification of the divine demands.[1]

Furthermore, the events with which Apocalyptic deals are 'mythological' events, in the strict sense in which, if I understand him aright, Professor Bultmann uses that term. That is to say, they are purely supernatural occurrences, belonging to the 'other side', which are *described* in the language of 'this side', in the categories of history. But they are not part of the natural fabric of history, relatable by any horizontal nexus of cause and effect to present historical events or predictable from them. They have a purely supernatural origin; they come 'out of the blue', and can be represented in the language of nature and history only in terms of the abnormal, the discontinuous and catastrophic.

This is in marked contrast with the interpretation given by the Prophets, the data for whose predictions and warnings are

[1] *Vide* T. W. Manson, 'Some Reflections on Apocalyptic', *Aux sources de la tradition chrétienne: Mélanges offerts à M. Goguel,* pp. 139–45.

the events and trends of ordinary history. These events may not be in any sense abnormal: they are often to be distinguished from other events only by the ultimate and decisive significance for the purpose of God which the Prophet declares them to possess. In order to represent this significance resort may be had to highly poetic or mythological language: history may, as it were, be cast into italics. But the reference of this language is always to events which have, or will have, their place in the historical series. The events may indeed be entirely predictable from current trends (as, for instance, was the fall of Jerusalem in the time of Jeremiah), and after them other events can be expected to occur without a break.

The Apocalyptist, on the other hand, is not primarily concerned with what a Nebuchadnezzar or a Cyrus may or may not do. It does not ultimately matter what they do. The kind of occurrences with which he deals do not have their origin within this order of events at all. They are inserted into history from without, by the sovereign power of God. And when they come, they come to wind history up. Life in the age to come is entirely discontinuous with life in this one. God does not act by using the historical event and through it fashioning his purpose for history. What the Apocalyptist looks to is the supersession of history as we know it altogether.

Now the effect of Dr Albert Schweitzer's unforgettable contribution to New Testament studies has been to obscure these distinctions. In phrases which after more than half a century still reverberate like a gong in our ears, he riveted upon our attention the crucial importance of the eschatological element in the teaching of Jesus. Yet throughout he interpreted eschatology in terms of the assumptions of late Jewish apocalyptic. And still today it is insufficiently recognized that Jesus' teaching may have been—as I am convinced it was—eschatological in its emphasis from beginning to end, without being apocalyptic in its basic outlook. Professor Kümmel, even though he believes that Jesus spoke of his return, goes so far as to say: 'The eschatological message of Jesus stands in complete contrast to the outlook of apocalyptic' (*Promise and*

Fulfilment, p. 104).[1] This is not to say that Jesus did not employ the language and the medium of apocalyptic; he certainly did,[2] though the effect of a critical scrutiny of the eschatological discourse of Mark 13 is undoubtedly in large degree, as Dr Vincent Taylor has said, to 'detach from his shoulders the glittering apocalyptic robe with which primitive Christianity clothed him, and with which he is still draped in popular Christian expectation' (*St Mark*, p. 644). But, however much or little he used of the language, it is the underlying assumptions that are decisive, and in these I believe Jesus had far more in common with the Prophets than with the Apocalyptic writers.

His concern was with the present moment, with the crisis introduced into history by the advent of the Kingdom of God, at work proleptically in his ministry and shortly to be 'fulfilled' in his death and vindication. Confronted by this, men were in the presence of the eschatological event, that final act of God in history, of which all the events of which the Prophets spoke were but the shadow cast before. Jesus was not interested in the future for its own sake; he was concerned to bring home to the Jewish nation the eternal consequences of this moment, alike in its offer and in its demands. Such was the purport of his parables and the challenge of his ethics.

It was not, as far as we can judge, that Jesus looked to God to introduce some catastrophic event, such as could only be

[1]Cf. M. Goguel: 'The thought of Jesus was eschatological; it was not apocalyptic' ('Eschatologie et apocalyptique dans le christianisme primitif', *Revue de l'histoire des religions*, CVI (1932), p. 387. Goguel traces the distinction between eschatology and apocalyptic right through the New Testament writings (op. cit., pp. 381–434, 489–524), but his definition of the terms is somewhat different.

[2]Cf. C. C. McCown, *The Promise of His Coming*, p. 154: 'The multitudes whom Jesus addressed, the disciples whom he chose, knew only the world view of the apocalyptist. Even if he chose to go back to the prophets and make use of their language and moral standards, he would have seemed to the people to use the language of apocalypticism, for the prophets were interpreted in an apocalyptic sense'. (I have reversed the order of the two sentences.)

J.C.–G

described in mythological terms and which would interrupt history and bring it to a close. Rather, he saw *in the historical events* mounting to a climax in his own rejection and death that through which God was working his decisive, messianic act. This act would have its historical consequences, like every other event in history, and some of these, he, like the Prophets, foresaw and included in the significance of the whole. To elucidate and bring home this significance he was prepared to employ any categories of interpretation familiar to his audience. Among them was that, deriving originally from the apocalyptic tradition, of the coming of the Son of man. To use such language was necessarily and deliberately to characterize these events as eschatological, of final consequence for God's people and their leaders. But it was not in itself to abandon historical expectation for something purely mythological. To say, with Schweitzer, that Jesus looked for, and indeed sought to compel, an act of God quite different from that which actually occurred and that he therefore died a broken and disappointed man is to make statements for which there is simply no evidence.

But what the early Church did was precisely to make this translation of the eschatology of Jesus into the thought-forms of apocalyptic. It is a process which can be traced throughout the development of the Synoptic tradition and which reaches its climax in the Gospel of Matthew. The eschatological language of Jesus is increasingly referred not to the historical crisis and climax of his ministry, but to a point beyond it, and to certain highly mythological occurrences expected after a gradually lengthening interval. As in Judaism earlier, the indissoluble unity between the ethical and the eschatological is severed. The 'ethics' of Jesus come to be separated out, detached from their eschatological setting, and adapted to the ordered life of the Church. In the same way, the eschatological elements are assembled and schematized to provide a map for the future and a programme for its hope.

This process finds its natural conclusion in the Sermon on the Mount of Matt. 5–7 on the one hand and the apocalyptic compendium of Matt. 24–5 on the other. But the stages of it may be illustrated in the three blocks in which the eschatological teaching of Jesus is to be found in the Gospel of Luke. The most developed state is to be seen in Luke 21, which, as it stands at present, is a fully articulated apocalypse, a formal discourse about the Last Things, with a beginning, middle and end. Luke 17.20–37, in contrast, is not so much a programme of the End as a flysheet or anthology of sayings grouped somewhat loosely about a common eschatological theme. But they are still sayings segregated by their subject-matter from other teaching. Finally, in Luke 11.49–13.9, we have a third block, which is not a self-contained section at all, so much as a sample dip into the Gospel material. It contains much of what elsewhere in the tradition is (or could well have been) collected under the heading of 'eschatology', but it is interspersed and integrated in the most natural way with other matter, much of which finds its way into Matthew's Sermon on the Mount and Mission Charge. This third sample of the tradition is, I believe, much nearer to what the mixture originally looked like before it was separated out: it is mostly early ('Q') material, and it is usually in its other contexts or versions that it shows the signs of secondary treatment.[1] Here the eschatological teaching of Jesus is no longer a separate subject, concerned with the future, remote or near. It relates to the urgency and finality which attaches to the whole of his mission and message, focused in the all-embracing announcement of the Kingdom of God, its coming, its carrier, and its claims.

It is not only the pervasive influence of St Matthew's Gospel, with its formal divisions of Jesus' teaching, which has tended to obscure this, but the assumptions also of much modern criticism. For both the Liberal school of 'the Jesus of history' and the exponents of 'thorough-going eschatology' took what might be described as the separation of the milk for granted. This is how they came to it, with the eschatological and the

[1]With 11.49–51 cf. Matt. 23.34–6; with 12.8 f. cf. Matt. 10.32 f.; Mark 8.38; with 12.31 f. cf. Matt. 6.33; with 12.57–9 cf. Matt. 5.25 f.; with 13.6–9 cf. Mark 11.13 f.

ethical teaching already standing at different levels. To Harnack and the Liberals it seemed possible to skim off the layer
of apocalyptic and still leave the pure milk of the gospel in the
Sermon on the Mount. Unfortunately, however, it is of the nature
of skimmed milk to be rather thin. Schweitzer and his followers, on the other hand, rightly regarding the eschatological
reference of Jesus' teaching as determinative, concentrated
solely upon the apocalyptic. Where they went wrong was in
assuming that where this was most rich, there the material was
most primitive. In fact, the crucial passages upon which their
case was grounded—the mission charge and the apocalyptic
discourse of Matthew—are among the most composite in the
Gospel tradition. So far from being the original cream of the
gospel, untouched by human hand, the Synoptic apocalypses
represent the teaching of Jesus already well seasoned, cooked
and labelled in the kitchens of the Mediterranean underworld
and tricked out in well-defined courses as 'food for the fed
up'.

To draw attention to this process of separation and to
question the primitive character of the apocalyptic strain in
the message of Jesus, is not (it must again be emphasized) to
say that Jesus himself taught a purely 'realized eschatology'
and that the futurist elements in the Gospel tradition are
simply the creation of the Church.

In this connexion, it is worth drawing attention to the
ambiguity which attaches to the phrase 'realized eschatology'
and to the confusion therefore which it is liable to introduce.
For there are two related senses in which the term has come to
be used, according to the context to which it is applied. The
first usage predominates in Dr Dodd's *Apostolic Preaching
and its Developments*, the second in his *Parables of the Kingdom*.

In the first sense, 'realized eschatology' represents the view
that the Kingdom of God comes fully and completely in the
historical crisis of the life, death and resurrection of Jesus,
and that none of his teaching refers to any coming subsequent
to this. In this sense no one stands for a more completely
realized eschatology than Schweitzer. For him (*The Mystery of*

the Kingdom of God, p. 124), the parables of watchfulness have no more reference to anything after this event than they have for Dodd; for, on his definition, nothing *can* happen after that final crisis. Or, rather, nothing should have happened after it —and to that extent Schweitzer represents the hope of Jesus as a completely unrealized eschatology: 'The death of Jesus is the end of eschatology!' (op. cit., p. 248).

But, in another sense, applied within the period of Jesus' life-time, the phrase is used to emphasize that the Kingdom was already a present fact *during the Ministry,* and not simply something to which he still looked forward. In this sense Schweitzer and Dodd represent opposite poles, Schweitzer believing that to the very end Jesus saw the Kingdom purely as a future event, Dodd that from the moment Jesus came into Galilee he proclaimed it as an existing reality.

In neither connexion, perhaps, is 'realized eschatology' the most felicitous expression. For the situation within the ministry of Jesus I should prefer to resort, if one has to, to some such term as 'proleptic eschatology'—to indicate that, while the Kingdom comes in power, and the hour of the Son of man arrives, only with the death of Jesus, yet the signs of the messianic age are already to be seen, in anticipation, 'before the time' (Matt. 8.29), in his words and deeds.[1]

For relating that hour to the future and to the final consummation of God's purpose, 'inaugurated eschatology' would appear the most satisfactory term. For at that hour *all* is inaugurated, yet *only* inaugurated. From then on that through which in the end the world must be saved or condemned comes finally into history: thenceforward men are in the presence of the eschatological event and the eschatological community.

All this, Jesus declared, was in the process of being set in motion; and, with the coming of the Passion, the great 'henceforth' could at last be pronounced. What, later, the Church proclaimed was, *not* that *all* was *inaugurated,* but that while

[1] *Vide* the positions reached both by Kümmel and by Fuller, op. cit.

some elements in it were now fulfilled, others still lay purely in the future. Those things which Jesus averred of his vindication were seen as accomplished: he had sat down at the right hand of God, angels and authorities and powers being subjected to him. Of what he spoke of his visitation, on the other hand, the great part was deferred for future, though still proximate, fulfilment. He *has* sat down, and he *will* come: such was the formula that emerged from the words at the Trial. And in the course of this process, the coming on the clouds, depicting originally, like the session at the right hand, his vindication before God, became assimilated to the other sayings about 'the coming of the Son of man', and with them was applied to a coming *from* God to be awaited by the Church, soon, suddenly and in great glory.

The process by which this change took place we have sought to indicate. Through the medium of apocalyptic, teaching of Jesus, given to bring home to his contemporaries the nature of the events in whose shadow they so carelessly lived, comes to be applied to the Church to alert it for his return. The single Event, *from* which the Christ reigns till all is subject to him, becomes two events, two halves of the messianic act, *between* which the Church lives and waits.

But before turning to the fundamental question of why this division should have occurred at all, we must pursue the trail of development further into the life of the Church. We have examined the position on both sides of the gulf, represented, schematically, by the year 30 and the year 50; and we have pointed to a process at work which may explain the transition from the one to the other. But can we narrow the gap any further?

In the opening chapter we detected some signs of a stage, reflected in the earliest preaching and credal summaries, at which the message of the Church itself was nearer to what we have reconstructed of the teaching of Jesus than to its subsequent *Parousia* hope. But we had then no means of assessing whether the apparent absence of the expectation might not represent simply a flaw in the transmission. That there should be such a lacuna in the evidence would indeed hardly be surprising, in view of the fact that there is no direct testimony at all for this first 'tunnel' period of the Church's history. But are we now in a position to say anything more? Can we, from the evidence of the Epistles or of the Gospels, probe behind the developed *Parousia* doctrine, not, this time, to the teaching of Jesus, but to the stage in the community tradition at which the conception emerged? How, and at what point, was the transition made *within* the thinking of the Church itself? Was it made from the very beginning? Or, if not, are the indications that it occurred nearer to the beginning or to the end of the 'silent' years?

In the chapter that follows we shall look at the evidence of the earliest Epistles. This evidence is by its very nature a challenge to the conclusion which our argument has reached. For if there was a development such as we have claimed to trace, the earliest *direct* evidence—that, namely, of the Thessalonian correspondence—reflects a situation where that development is not only already over but has, apparently, disappeared without trace. This is bound once again to raise the question whether it really took place at all; and it means that we shall be compelled to go into the earliest Pauline evidence in some detail.

But, as we shall see, if the evidence of the Gospels cannot be isolated from that of the Epistles, so neither can that of the Epistles be isolated from the Gospel tradition. Both are equally important testimony to the processes going on within the thinking and theology of the earliest Church. Consequently, in the subsequent chapter we shall return once more to the Synoptic material. But, on this occasion, it will not be to trace the transition from the expectation of Jesus to that of the Church, but to try to discover the process within the Church's own expectation which lies behind the admitted, but still unexplained, fact that upon its very first appearance in Thessalonians the *Parousia* doctrine bursts upon us, not in bud, but already in full and luxuriant flower.

THE CHALLENGE OF THESSALONIANS

In the previous chapter we described the change that came over the teaching of Jesus as it went through the process of transmission by the Church as comparable with the transition within the Old Testament from Prophecy to Apocalyptic. But the objection can be raised that this reconstruction, which might be arguable from the Gospels alone, breaks down on the evidence outside the Gospels. In particular, there is the fact that in I and II Thessalonians, at a date earlier than any of our Gospels, is to be found eschatological material, having affinities with that in the Gospels, which is as highly apocalyptic as anything in the Synoptists. What is there reflected of the teaching of Jesus is already completely integrated into a fully-developed *Parousia* doctrine. And there is no sign that it ever had any other reference. Moreover, from the evidence of the Pauline Epistles it is usually held that the line of development, if there was one, was precisely in the opposite direction—*away*, that is to say, from a primitive apocalyptic outlook to something less apocalyptic.

This I believe to be a correct assessment of the Pauline evidence. But the question has still to be asked, whatever the development in Paul's thinking between, say, A.D. 50 and 60, whether the apocalyptic outlook was itself really primitive. Can the testimony of Thessalonians show that this interpretation, and with it the *Parousia* hope in its established form, went back, if not to Jesus himself, at any rate to a point beyond that at which the Gospel tradition can be used as evidence to the contrary? For, if so, any conclusions hitherto derived from the Gospels would be undercut.

The answer to the question is, I believe, in the negative. Despite its chronological priority, the material in Thessalonians cannot take us back behind, nor call in question, the transition into apocalyptic which the Gospel material indicates. This is the kind of statement which if it is to be worth anything must be established in some detail. But it may be helpful to summarize in advance the substance of the argument.

It will be argued that, of the eschatological material in Thessalonians, the more apocalyptic the passage, the remoter is its connexion with anything in the Gospel tradition which may claim to be primitive or provide evidence for the teaching of Jesus. What connexion there is—and much of it is more apparent than real—is with elements in that tradition that can be shown to be secondary. Their occurrence in Thessalonians proves, not that they are not secondary, but that the tendencies which produced them set in much earlier than the Gospels by themselves would lead us to expect. Already, it appears, by the year 50, the Church was thinking in a manner reflected in the Synoptic material only in its latest strands. In other words, the Gospel tradition of the teaching of Jesus remained unaffected by these tendencies for a considerably longer time than it would have done had it simply mirrored the contemporary theology of the Church. There is evidence of a time-lag, a resistance to purely ecclesiastical motifs, which actually strengthens rather than undermines our confidence in the Gospel tradition.

On the other hand, the less apocalyptic the eschatological material in Thessalonians, the closer appears to be its connexion with the Gospel tradition, and with those strata of it which, on the basis of Synoptic criticism, may be regarded as most primitive. But, here again, we shall find that in the matter of secondary developments the Gospel material is at least as pure as, if not purer than, the corresponding passages in Thessalonians, despite the chronological priority of the latter. The fact, therefore, that by the time of Thessalonians sayings have already been given the same reference to the *Parousia* that they carry in the Gospels cannot be used to prove that such an application was the original one, if there are other grounds for doubting it. It shows only how soon this application came to be made. And, again, it is testimony to the faithfulness of the Gospel tradition that at the date at which the Gospels were composed there should still be traces of a different reference, all signs of which have already been covered in the Church's own thinking, as represented by I and II Thessalonians.

In support of these conclusions, we may begin by plunging straight into the highly coloured apocalyptic passages of I Thess. 4.13–18 and II Thess. 1.6–2.12.

The possible parallels with the Gospel tradition may be set out as follows:

(*a*) I Thess. 4.15: *the coming* of the Lord

Matt. 24.27: *the coming* of the Son of man

(*b*) I Thess. 4.16: the *trumpet* of God

Matt. 24.31: with a great *trumpet*

(*c*) I Thess. 4.17: we . . . shall be caught up together with them *in the clouds to meet* the Lord

Mark 13.26: the Son of man coming *in clouds*

Matt. 25.6: Come out *to meet* him

(*d*) II Thess. 1.6–10: to *repay* with affliction those who afflict you . . . at the revelation of the Lord Jesus from heaven *with the angels of his* power, inflicting *vengeance* . . . *when* he *comes* on that day to be *glorified* in his holy ones

Matt. 16.27: For the Son of man is to come *with his angels* in the *glory* of his Father, and then he will *repay* every man for what he has done

Matt. 25.31: *When* the Son of man *comes* in his *glory*, and all *the angels with him*

Luke 21.22: These are days of *vengeance*

(*e*) II Thess. 2.1: our *gathering together* to him

Mark 13.27: he will . . . *gather* the elect *together*

(*f*) II Thess. 2.3f.: the son of perdition . . . who takes his seat in the temple of God

Matt. 24.15: the desolating sacrilege . . . standing in the holy place

(g) II Thess. 2.7: the mystery of *lawlessness* is already at work	Matt. 24.12: because *lawlessness* is multiplied
(h) II Thess. 2.9 f.: the coming of the lawless one . . . will be with all power and with *false signs and wonders,* and with all wicked deception.	Mark 13.22: *False* Christs and *false* prophets will arise and will show *signs and wonders,* to lead astray.

From this list two things emerge.

In the first place, a large proportion of the echoes occur in quotations from the Old Testament. They cannot therefore be used to establish any direct link between the two documents. There is nothing to show that Paul or the kind of thinking he represents is here reproducing any tradition of the words of Jesus. All that can be said is that both apocalypses draw at points upon a common stock of established eschatological symbolism.[1] In no case is there a direct citation from the same source; and, in view of the fact that parts of both apocalypses are pastiches of Old Testament quotations, their independence is quite as remarkable as their occasional resemblance.

[1]Thus, in (b), the trumpet as a sign of the End goes back to such passages as Isa. 27.12 f. (from which Matthew appears to be quoting), Joel 2.1 and IV Ezra 6.23; cf. I Cor. 15.52. In (c), the imagery of the clouds as a natural vehicle of ascent to God is to be found in Dan. 7.13; IV Ezra 13.3; II Enoch 3.1; etc. In (d), there can be no case for dependence upon the Synoptic tradition for the Lord coming to exact vengeance and retribution, when comparison is made with Isa. 66.15, to which Paul's words ἐν πυρὶ φλογός, διδόντος ἐκδίκησιν are a clear allusion. Again, in II Thess. 1.9 f., the phrase, 'from the presence of the Lord and from the glory of his might, when he comes . . . on that day' is an almost exact quotation of the LXX of Isa. 2.19 f.; and the remainder of v. 10 is echoed from Pss. 89.7 and 67.36 (LXX). In (e), the ingathering of the saints at the consummation is, as we have seen, a commonplace of Old Testament prophecy (cf. especially Isa. 27.12 f., where it is joined with the blowing of the great trumpet). In (h), the only common phrasing between II Thess. 2.9 and Mark 13.22 occurs in the latter's echo of Deut. 13.1, where the false prophet is to give a sign and a wonder with intent to deceive, which again is a recognized feature of the End-time (e.g. Orac. Sib. 3, 66–70).

The second fact that emerges is that, where there are simi-
larities with the Gospel tradition which do not occur simply
in quotations, it is with elements in it that cannot claim to take
us back to Jesus himself or even to any very early period in the
Church's thinking. In every case the contact is found to be
with Matthean material only, and that belonging to the last,
editorial stage, which must be regarded as among the latest
matter in the Synoptic tradition.

Thus, in (*a*), there is the use of the term *parousia* itself. Its
occurrence in the Gospels is confined, as we have seen, to four
verses in Matt. 24. On its first appearance in v. 3, it is palpably
introduced by the Evangelist into his Markan material, in order
to make Jesus' words about the destruction of Jerusalem apply,
as the subsequent discourse demands, to the second coming
and the end of the world. In vv. 27, 37, and 39 the phrase 'the
parousia of the Son of man' occurs in 'Q' material from which
it is absent in Luke. Even if the Lucan equivalents are themselves not original, it would obviously be highly precarious to
argue that Matthew's terminology went back to Jesus or even
to 'Q'. Consequently, the use of the word *parousia* in the
Thessalonian correspondence can inspire no more confidence
that it reflects the actual usage of Jesus than its other terms,
'the revelation', 'the manifestation', or 'the day', of Christ,
which are not represented in the Gospel tradition but which
recur in the later Epistles.

Further, the association, in (*d*), of the *Parousia* with retribution is to be found in the Gospels only in Matthew, where
it is evidently a secondary and editorial development. The
clearest instance of this is one we have already noted, where
the closing phrase of Mark 8.38, 'when he comes in the glory
of his Father with the holy angels', is further elaborated in
Matt. 16.27 to:

'the Son of man is to come with his angels in the glory of his Father,
and then he will repay every man for what he has done.'

The idea of retribution is also combined by Matthew with that
of the coming of the Son of man in the mourning of the tribes

of the earth in 24.30 (an addition to Mark) and in the vision of
the Last Assize in 25.31–46.[1] In the earlier strands of the
Synoptic tradition the triumph of the Son of man is associated
with vindication and rejection, but not specifically with retribution and punishment. The later connexion is to be ex-
plained, both in Matthew and in Paul, not by reference to
Jesus, but by the regular occurrence of this element in the
theophanies of the Old Testament, which came in Christianity
to be applied to the *Parousia*.

Of all the links between Thessalonians and the Gospel
tradition the most striking is perhaps the association, in (*d*), of
the Lord Jesus at his *Parousia* with 'the angels of his power'.
The closest parallel is provided once again by Matt. 16.27,
where the Son of man is to come 'with his angels'. But as in
other respects, so here this verse shows the signs of being the
end term of a considerable development. Going back to what
we took to be the most original form of the saying on which it
is based, we have in the 'Q' tradition of Luke 12.9 the words:
'He who denies me before men will be denied before *the angels
of God*'. In Mark 8.38 this last phrase is expanded to the clause,
'when he comes *in the glory of his Father with the holy angels*'.
Luke at this point (9.26) has '*in his glory and the glory of the
Father and of the holy angels*', while Matthew, as we have seen,
substitutes: '*with his* [i.e., the Son of man's] *angels in the glory
of his Father*'. There is a progressive detachment both of the
glory and of the angels of the Son from those of the Father.
That this is not fortuitous, at any rate in Matthew, is shown by
the change which he makes again in the following verse (16.28),
when he alters Mark's 'See that the kingdom of God has come
with power' to 'See the Son of man coming in *his* kingdom'.
Similarly, in Matthew's allegorization of the parable of the
Tares, we have: 'The Son of man will send out *his* angels, and
they will gather out of *his* kingdom all causes of sin and all evil
doers' (13.41). Finally, it is to be noted that in his apocalypse
Matthew twice more inserts a 'his' into the Markan account,

[1]Cf. also the Matthean application of the parables of the Tares and
the Dragnet in 13.40–2 and 49 f.

appropriating the angels of the *Parousia,* and the elect, expressly to the Son of man (24.31). Whereas in the earlier tradition the angels are thought of as being entirely at the Father's disposal and the adjuncts of his splendour, later the Son has his own celestial force and his independent glory. It is therefore worth observing how in Thessalonians the Lord Jesus is to be revealed from heaven with 'the angels of *his* power'. The contact of Thessalonians is again with the latest rather than with the earliest state of the Synoptic tradition.

It is also perhaps noteworthy that in Thessalonians the coming of the Lord is described unambiguously as a descent *from* heaven (I Thess. 1.10; 4.16; II Thess. 1.7). It was argued earlier that the coming on the clouds denoted originally a coming *to* God and that it is only in secondary passages in the Synoptic tradition that it must be understood as describing the reverse process. Even in these passages it is only implied, not stated, that the movement is from heaven; but it is again perhaps significant that this is least ambiguous in Matthew, whose addition of the sign of the Son of man 'in heaven' prior to his 'coming' (24.30) provides once more the nearest parallel to the language of Thessalonians.

There are only three parallels not yet accounted for. None is of serious importance, but in each case the affinity is again with phrases which occur solely in the first Gospel. Matthew alone among the Evangelists uses the word 'lawlessness', to be found in (*g*); and as a description of the End-time (cf. IV Ezra 5.2; I Enoch 91.5–7) it occurs in a verse which he has himself inserted into the Markan apocalypse (24.12). In so far as there is any real parallel in (*f*), it is because Matthew has added specific mention of the Temple to the quotation from Dan. 11.31, just as Paul himself has introduced it into his echoes of Dan. 11.36 and Ezek. 28.2. At this point Matthew cannot claim to be a witness to the words of Jesus. He is clearly secondary to Mark, whose version, we shall argue,[1] is itself inferior at this point to the tradition preserved in Luke 21.20. Lastly, the occurrence, in (*c*), of the regular phrase for 'coming

[1] *Vide* p. 122 below.

to meet'[1] could hardly be considered of any significance, were it not for the *Parousia* context in which Matthew has placed the parable of the Virgins.[2] There is no evidence that it is in itself a technical eschatological term, pointing to a common tradition,[3] but once again the contact, if any, is with the Matthean material.

This affinity with Matthew, and that not with the special source behind his material, but with the latest and editorial elements in the Gospel, must be allowed full weight.[4] In his book, *St Paul's Conceptions of the Last Things*, H. A. A. Kennedy wrote: 'It is no exaggeration to say that Matt. 24 is the most instructive commentary on the chapter before us [II Thess. 2]' (p. 56). In a sense very different from that in which he meant it, it is certainly an instructive commentary that it should be this most highly elaborated specimen of Gospel apocalypse that has the greatest affinities with Thessalonians. For it indicates that the contact of the Epistles, at any rate in their apocalyptic sections, is not with material that might take us nearer to the original teaching of Jesus but with tendencies recognizably secondary to such authentic tradition as we already possess.

We turn now to the other material in Thessalonians which, while undoubtedly eschatological, is not in itself apocalyptic. It is not, that is to say, concerned with the 'unveiling' or depicting of forthcoming events of a supernatural character. It

[1]Cf. Acts 28.15, of the Christians of Rome going out to meet Paul.
[2]For its original setting cf. p. 69 above.
[3]It is carefully discussed by J. Dupont in his study ΣΥΝ ΧΡΙΣΤΩΙ: *L'Union avec le Christ suivant Saint Paul. Première partie,* pp. 64–73. Like others, he draws attention to the modelling of I Thess. 4. 15–17 upon the theophany on Sinai in Ex. 19.10–18, where the phrase εἰς συνάντησιν occurs. In this case, it should be included rather under our first heading, of Old Testament echoes.
[4]It is recognized, and indeed pressed to exaggeration, by J. Orchard, in his article, 'Thessalonians and the Synoptic Gospels', in *Biblica*, XIX (1938), pp. 19–42. But his inference, that Paul knew Matt. 23.31–25.46 and that 'this passage is something absolutely

focuses attention rather on the response within history to a situation of final and decisive significance—upon the existential rather than the mythological. This material is, of course, closely integrated with the apocalyptic material, and its teaching is applied by Paul to the supra-historical event of the *Parousia*. For him, that is to say, the distinction is an artificial one: in Thessalonians, as in certain strands of the Synoptic tradition, the eschatological has already been thoroughly 'apocalypticized'. But this must not be allowed to prejudge the question whether this material may not previously have possessed a different and non-apocalyptic reference, and have had its original application not to the *Parousia* but to a crisis in the historical order. What makes it worth while to press this distinction between the eschatological and apocalyptic is not only the validity which it has been found to possess in relation to the Gospels, but the fact that when it is applied here it yields interesting and significant results. For, in this second kind of material, the affinities are with very different strata of the Synoptic tradition, which have much greater claim to embody the teaching of Jesus than those we have so far considered. In short, the parallels here are with 'Q', Mark, and the special Lucan source, whereas previously they were with editorial elements in Matthew.

Among this material, brief reference may first be made to what could be a reminiscence of the words of Jesus in the highly apocalyptic passage we have just been discussing. This occurs not in the portrayal of the coming events themselves— where we have detected no genuine echo of Jesus' teaching— but in the attitude which is to be adopted to them. In II Thess. 2.2 f. Paul warns his converts: 'Do not be alarmed. . . . Let no one deceive you.' This has affinities with the 'Do not be

primordial and must be dated somewhere between 40 and 50 A.D.' (p. 39), flies in the face of Synoptic criticism and the evident dependence of the Matthean apocalypse in its present form on Mark 13 and other sources. Rigaux, op. cit., pp. 95–105, rejects Orchard's position, but does not give sufficient recognition to the Matthean contacts.

alarmed' and 'Take heed that no one leads you astray' of Mark
13.7 and 5. But while the injunctions themselves are similar, the
occasions which call them forth are not the same. In Mark the
reference is to the historical scene, to wars and the appearance
of messianic pretenders; in II Thessalonians it is to the rumour
that the day of the Lord, with the *Parousia* and the ingathering
of the saints, has already set in. In assessing which of these two
is the more likely to represent the original reference, account
must be taken of the fact that, while the situations for which
Jesus prepares the disciples in Mark 13.5–13 are to be paralleled elsewhere in his teaching,[1] the context in II Thess. 2
affords, as we have seen, no other parallels of his words. Despite the chronological priority, therefore, of Thessalonians,
the application given to the warnings in the Gospel tradition
must be judged nearer to the outlook of Jesus.

The decisive passage in this connexion is, however, that of
I Thess. 5.1–11. The theme is the need for watchfulness, and
there is at least one almost certain reference to a saying of
Jesus, namely, to the parable of the Burglar recorded in 'Q'
(Luke 12.39 f.=Matt. 24.43 f.).[2] This is alluded to as part of a
tradition with which the Thessalonians are familiar:

'As to the times and the seasons, brethren, you have no need to have
anything written to you. For you yourselves know well that the day
of the Lord will come as a thief in the night.'

There then follows a passage containing echoes of the sayings
which now form the close of the Markan and Lucan apocalypses:

[1] Mark 13.21–3; Luke 12.11 f.; 17.23; 19.43 f.; 21.12–19 (probably independent of Mark); 23.28–31; cf. John 14.25–31.

[2] Cf. Jeremias, op. cit., p. 40: 'The symbol of the thief is frequently
employed in early Christian literature, and, since it is foreign to the
eschatological imagery of late Jewish literature, we may infer that
the passages in which it is found are based on the parable of Jesus'.
It is used in Joel 2.9 of the hosts that are to consume the land on
the day of the Lord. 'They climb up into the houses, they enter
through the windows like a thief'. But here the simile has nothing to
do with suddenness.

J.C.—H

I Thess. 5.3–7	Luke 21.34–6
When they say, 'There is peace and security', then *sudden destruction* will *come upon* them as travail comes upon a woman with child, and there will be no *escape*. But you are not in darkness, brethren, for *that day* to surprise you like a thief. . . . So then let us not sleep, as others do, but let us *keep awake* and be sober. For those who *sleep* sleep at night, and those who get *drunk* are drunk at night.	But take heed to yourselves lest your hearts be weighed down with dissipation and *drunkenness* and cares of this life, and *that day come upon* you *suddenly* like a snare. . . . But watch at all times, praying that you may have strength to *escape* all these things that will take place.

Mark 13.35 f.
Keep awake therefore . . . lest he come suddenly and find you *asleep*.

The parallels here, in contrast with those previously considered, are not in quotations from Scripture, nor are they to be found in what are evidently secondary strata of the Gospel material. It looks as if we have genuine echoes of a common tradition, and one which has strong claim to embody elements of the teaching of Jesus himself.

As in the corresponding passages in the Gospels, this language is by Paul referred to the *Parousia*. But here too we must be prepared to employ the tests we applied to the Synoptic material, to discover what in it is really primitive.

The stress laid upon the suddenness of coming disaster we found to be a characteristic of the earliest stratum of the teaching of Jesus, and one tending to be overlaid by other motifs in the developing tradition. The unadorned simile which Paul uses to express this, 'as a pang upon a woman with child', has the same authentic ring as that of the closing of the trap in Luke 21.34, and both may well go back to sayings of Jesus.[1] Elsewhere in the Old and New Testaments the pangs of birth

---

[1] J. B. Lightfoot regarded it as 'not unlikely' that the whole of v.3 ('When they say, "There is peace and security", then sudden destruction will come upon them as travail comes upon a woman with child, and there will be no escape') is 'a direct quotation from our Lord's words' and that 'the reference implied in the word αὐτοῖς is to be sought for in the context of the saying from which St Paul

are always a symbol not of suddenness but of anguish,[1] and the natural tendency would have been to draw out the analogy in this direction.

On the other hand, the process of allegorization is well advanced, which in the Gospel parables is to be regarded as a sign of subsequent development. For Paul the thief comes 'in the night,'[2] and upon this detail he elaborates allegorically, though, as so often in his metaphors, not very consistently. The point is significant for him because Christians are children not of darkness but of the light, and should therefore not be overtaken as by a thief, nor should they be caught drunk or asleep, both of which are states belonging to the night. But as a result of his allegorization the metaphor breaks in his hands, and what begins as a symbol of darkness ends inconsequentially as a figure for 'the Day': 'You are not in darkness, brethren, that *the day* should overtake you like a thief'.[3] Precisely by its application to the *Parousia* the original figure is destroyed.

It is clear that once Paul leaves the simple parable he is not trustworthy evidence for the tradition behind his words. As a matter of fact, we may be able to reconstruct that tradition from an unexpected source. In John 12.35 f. there is the same contrast between the sons of light and those who walk in darkness, but this time with the injunction: 'Walk while you

---

quotes' (*Notes on the Epistles of St Paul*, p. 72). The words would fit easily enough into some such context as Luke 17.26–32.

[1] Isa. 13.8; 21.3; 26.17; Jer. 6.24; 13.21; Mic. 4.9 f. etc.; Mark 13.8 and 17; John 16.21 f.

[2] There is nothing to suggest this in Luke 12.39. It is implied by the words, 'he would have kept awake', of Matt. 24.43; but this touch is almost certainly a Matthean addition to provide a link with the γρηγορεῖτε of the previous verse.

[3] Reading κλέπτης. If the variant reading κλέπτας is adopted ('that the day should surprise you as it does thieves'), the identification of the burglar with the deeds of darkness is preserved, but he then becomes the *object* of the surprise, and the picture is again changed.

have the light, that *darkness* may not overtake you'. This is
precisely what Paul should have written if he was to maintain
the metaphor, and this may well represent the underlying
tradition. Moreover, the fourth Gospel—and later we shall
have reason to conclude that this is not fortuitous—not only
appears to have retained the original form of the saying but
may well supply its original setting. Both in the Synoptists and
in Paul the parable is applied to the *Parousia*. In the former,
there are grounds for thinking this application to be secondary,[1] and in the latter we have seen that precisely this is the
source of the dislocation. In John the reference of the saying is
not to the *Parousia* but to the imminent climax of the ministry
of Jesus in the lifting up of the Son of man and the judgement
which that must bring (12.31-4). And it is in view of this that
Jesus says: 'The light is with you (only) for a little longer.
Walk while you have the light, lest the darkness overtake you.'
This is exactly the situation to which we argued that the other
parables of crisis were spoken before they were transferred to
a future coming.[2]

While, therefore, there is good reason to think that in
I Thess. 5.1–11 Paul preserves genuine echoes of the words of
Jesus, it is just at the point where this material is given its
apocalyptic application that our confidence wanes. Thessalonians can provide no firm ground for supposing that such
teaching referred originally to the *Parousia*. Nor, of course,
can it prove the opposite, since there is no suggestion of an
alternative reference. To decide the question, we are thrown
back once more on the Gospel tradition. What Paul can tell us
is that the Church had already by that date come to associate
its own *Parousia* hope with the words and parables of Jesus
and to read these in that light. But the fact that the Gospels

[1]Cf. pp. 69, 79 above and Jeremias, op. cit., pp. 39–41.

[2]*Vide* my article, 'The Parable of John 10.1–5', *Zeitschrift für die
Neutestamentiche Wissenschaft*, XLVI (1955), pp. 233–40. I there
argue that John 10.1–3a is another such parable of warning to the
Jews, centring upon the figure of the porter, and comparable with
the other parable of the porter, in Mark 13.34–6, *before* that was
referred to the *Parousia*.

hint, where Paul does not, at a stage behind that association is further testimony to the value of their tradition. What is remarkable, surely, is not that they should reflect so frequently the expectation of their writers, but that they should still retain traces of an alternative application, which, as much as a generation before, have already disappeared from the Pauline Epistles.

To repeat, then, what was said at the beginning, the conclusion is that the more apocalyptic the material in Thessalonians the less claim it has to represent primitive tradition, and *vice versa*. In view of this it would clearly be dangerous to argue that the application of Jesus' teaching to an apocalyptic *Parousia* must be original because it appears so unequivocally in our earliest documents. Certainly, as we have said, the material in these Epistles alone would give us no reason to challenge this reference. But if it is seriously questioned on the basis of the Gospel evidence, then the Thessalonian correspondence cannot be held to provide decisive testimony to the contrary. Indeed, its witness has tended to strengthen rather than diminish our trust in the Gospel tradition.

But we are still no nearer to discovering the stage in the Church's thinking at which the conception of the *Parousia* emerged. By the time of the earliest Pauline writings, the expectation is already there in as fully developed a form as it was ever to attain within the New Testament. Thereafter the problem shifted to the *delay* of that which in itself was clearly defined, and to the relation between what were subsequently to be designated the *two Parousias*. But can nothing be said of the process and the stages by which it came to that rapid maturity in the earliest years of the Church's life? If we cannot get behind Paul, are we in any better position to get behind the Evangelists?

THE EMERGENCE OF THE PAROUSIA DOCTRINE

IF the apocalypse of Thessalonians provides no hints of the development which went before it, that in the Gospels would appear to have left so many that almost every investigator can arrive at a different reconstruction.[1]

In the welter of competing views two things at any rate are beyond dispute. First, the eschatology of the Gospel of Mark as it now stands is dominated, and must be interpreted, by the apocalypse in chapter 13; and, secondly, the eschatology of chapter 13 is in its turn dominated, and must be interpreted, by the culminating paragraph on the *Parousia* in vv. 24–7:

'But in those days, after that tribulation, the sun will be darkened, and the moon will not give its light and the stars will be falling from heaven, and the powers in the heavens will be shaken. And then they will see the Son of man coming in clouds with great power and glory. And then he will send out the angels, and gather the elect from the four winds, from the ends of the earth to the ends of heaven.'

And what is true of Mark is true both of Matthew and Luke: any reference to the End must be understood in the light of their concluding apocalypse, and any reference to the 'coming' of the Son of man must be interpreted by the vision of the *Parousia* which marks its climax.

Now we had little hesitation earlier[2] in dismissing this paragraph as evidence for the teaching of Jesus himself: it clearly appeared to be a secondary compilation, reflecting the expecta-

[1]For a survey, cf. again Beasley-Murray, op. cit.
[2]Pp. 56 f. above.

tion of the early Church. But our present question is rather different. How does it stand towards the rest of the eschatology of the *Evangelists* which it now dominates? If, as we argued, it is secondary material in relation, say, to the Trial saying of Mark 14.62, at what point did it enter the tradition? Is it secondary also to the remainder of Mark 13, so that without it the rest of that chapter could provide evidence of an earlier stage, and thus perhaps throw light on the emergence of the *Parousia* hope in which it now culminates? Or was it from the beginning an integral part of this eschatological material—as of the Thessalonian apocalypse—so that here again there would be no intermediate stage to be seen between the original teaching of Jesus and the fully developed doctrine, represented in this paragraph substantially as in Thessalonians?

In such a matter there can be no question of final proof, if only because there is no extant document prior to Mark 13 in its present form. Any progress must be by way of hypothesis. But of the two hypotheses—and both are hypotheses—namely, that the *Parousia* hope was a part of this eschatological discourse from its initial compilation, and, secondly, that it was incorporated into it at a later stage—of these, the latter alternative has, I believe, much more to commend it.

In the first place, the paragraph Mark 13.24–7 stands out as containing, in comparison with the rest of the chapter, a uniquely low proportion of teaching that may reasonably be attributed to Jesus himself. It would be too great a digression to work through the whole of Mark 13 to substantiate this statement. Reference may be made to the very judicious assessment of the material given by Dr Vincent Taylor in his commentary on St Mark.[1] While there are secondary features and editorial touches to be detected throughout the chapter, there is elsewhere within it almost always ground for supposing that beneath the surface lies some teaching deriving from Jesus himself. But in this paragraph there is really no ground for such a supposition. Indeed, as we have seen,[2] the whole of it

[1] Ad loc. and Appendix E, pp. 636–44.
[2] Pp. 56 f. above.

virtually is a collection of Scriptural allusions, worked into a mosaic which it is most improbable that he himself composed.

Moreover, whereas the rest of the discourse, before and after, is addressed to the disciples in the second person, this paragraph alone is marked by an unexplained transition to the third person plural. The previous section begins: 'But when you see the desolating sacrilege . . .'; but in v. 26 it has become, for no apparent reason: 'Then *they* will see the Son of man coming in clouds'. This reads very much like the written style of an apocalypse inserted into a spoken discourse.

Furthermore, the verses interrupt the sequence of the argument. In vv. 28 f.,

'So also when you see these things taking place, know that he (it) is near, at the very gates,'

the lesson of the parable requires that 'these things' refer to signs *preceding* the End. But as the discourse stands, they must refer to the *Parousia* and the final ingathering itself, which fails to make sense; for it is no good being warned that it is near, even very near, at the actual moment of its occurrence. Without the paragraph of vv. 24–7, however, there is an excellent connexion with the premonitory events of vv. 14–20.

But the real test of the hypothesis is what happens if this paragraph is extracted.

What remains is (*a*) a connected discourse predicting a period of intense suffering culminating in the collapse of the nation and the destruction of Jerusalem (vv. 5–23);[1] and (*b*) a series of isolated sayings and parables which, as we saw,[2] have parallels in widely separated parts of the tradition (vv. 28–37).

---

[1]The closing vv. 21–3 appear to be another version of sayings already represented in vv. 5 f. and paralleled again in Luke 17.23. The real conclusion of the section is reached at v. 20. Luke has omitted them in his discourse at this point, and they will be left on one side in the discussion that follows.

[2]P. 86 above.

It is with the former section that we are chiefly concerned. For without the paragraph on the *Parousia* to which it now leads up, has it any longer any coherence or climax? Could it have formed a unit capable of existing on its own? This must be asked without prejudice to the question whether it was spoken by Jesus as a unit—or indeed by Jesus at all. The present issue is simply whether in structure it is so dependent upon its present culmination in the *Parousia* vision as to have no likelihood of circulation without it. If this were so, then the *Parousia* could not justifiably be regarded as a later or additional element.

In fact, the unit with which we are left not only retains an excellent structure but is actually more homogeneous than the discourse as it now stands. The connexion between the apocalyptic climax and the apparently purely historical warnings and predictions which precede it has always been problematical. Above all, in Mark, the discourse in its present form does not answer the question to which it is addressed. The disciples inquire about the destruction of the Temple and how they are to know when it is coming (13.1–4): Jesus replies about the end of the world and his own advent—a discrepancy of which Matthew shows himself fully aware by altering the question to fit the answer (24.3).

But, taking Mark 13.5–20 by itself, we have a perfectly consistent reply which falls into three sections, each taking up the question raised by the disciples, 'When will this be?' The first two paragraphs are negative, the third positive. '*When* you hear of wars and rumours of wars—do not be alarmed; for there will be many alarms and excursions before the final destruction comes (vv. 5–8); *when* you yourselves are arrested —do not be anxious; for there will be much to endure before the end (vv. 9–13); *but, when* you see the desolating sacrilege set up where it ought not to be—then take instant action; for this will be the time to make good your escape from the City (vv. 14–20).'

This discourse may well owe its present structure to the Church rather than to Jesus himself, and it is undoubtedly influenced by secondary motifs.[1] In particular, I believe that those are right who see in the reference to the abomination of desolation, with its cryptic note, 'Let the reader understand', an apocalypticizing of a straightforward historical reference, such as is preserved in the (independent and more original) tradition of Luke 21.20: 'But when you see Jerusalem surrounded by armies, then know that its desolation has come near.'[2] In any case, it is clear from the instructions that follow (Mark 13.14b–18) that the destruction of Jerusalem and the collapse of Judaea is what is in mind.

Thus reconstructed, the discourse ceases to be an apocalypse in any proper sense of the term. It is rather a solemn warning in the manner of the Prophets of the historical consequences of Israel's rejection and of the attitude which the faithful must adopt to them.

Now this is precisely what we concluded earlier[3] to be the original character of the similar discourse in Luke 17.22–37, which has also become conflated with extraneous material and applied to the *Parousia*. If, then, the original core of Mark 13 was such as we have argued, it no longer stands by itself as the unique phenomenon that it now is in the Gospel record. It represents the kind of instruction which circulated in at least two independent traditions.

But this is not all. It is likely that there is yet a third composition of this character, to be found in the parallel to the Markan discourse preserved in Luke 21. We have just suggested, in connexion with the abomination of desolation, that Luke is at this point using a version which is not dependent on

[1]E.g., 'the end' in vv. 7 and 13 must now refer to the end of the world, not the end of the nation; and v. 10 ('And the gospel must first be preached to all nations'), whose vocabulary is 'wholly and distinctively Markan' (Taylor, ad loc.), must be regarded as part of the same redaction.

[2]*Vide* C. H. Dodd, 'The Fall of Jerusalem and the "Abomination of Desolation",' *Journal of Roman Studies*, XXXVII (1947), pp. 47–54; cf. V. Taylor, op. cit., p. 512; T. W. Manson, *The Sayings of Jesus*, pp. 329 f.

[3]Pp. 73–7 above.

Mark, as previously we suspected also of his Passion narrative.[1] The arguments for this view have been set out by others[2] and are, I believe, convincing. What needs to be underlined is simply their consequences for the character of the original Lucan discourse.

The points at which in chapter 21 Luke is incorporating Markan material are fairly clearly defined, and, by simply omitting these verses, it is not difficult to reconstruct a coherent discourse of the very kind we have already identified in Mark 13 and Luke 17:[3]

[1]P. 50 above.

[2]A. M. Perry, *The Sources of St Luke's Passion Narrative*, pp. 35–8; V. Taylor, *Behind the Third Gospel*, pp. 109–25; T. W. Manson, op. cit., pp. 323–37; Beasley-Murray, op. cit., pp. 226 f.

[3]The beginning of the special Lucan source may be indicated by the redundant 'Then he said to them' of v. 10, but vv. 10 and 11 themselves are Markan. It is possible that the non-Markan matter in vv. 25b–26a describing the distress of nations and the foreboding at what is coming upon earth, introduced somewhat incongruously into the purely celestial setting of the *Parousia* paragraph, is in fact the Lucan opening displaced in vv. 10 and 11 by the Markan equivalent. But in its present order, Luke's own material probably begins at v. 12. Vv. 16 (probably) and 17 are from Mark. As the passage stands, there is a contradiction between 16b ('some of you they will put to death') and 18 ('not a hair of your head will perish'); but without vv. 16 and 17 an excellent connection is restored. V. 21a is Markan, and its insertion makes 'those who are in the midst of *her*' relate to Judaea, whereas here and at the end of the verse the pronoun must for its sense refer back to Jerusalem in v. 20. V. 23a is evidently taken from Mark as are 25a, 26b–27, and 29–33. The present connection at v.28 is very difficult ('They will see the Son of man coming in a cloud with power and great glory. But when *these things* begin to take place, look up and raise your heads, because your redemption is drawing near'). Without the *Parousia* paragraph, however, it follows admirably on v. 24. Alternatively, if something like 25b–26a represented the original opening of the Lucan discourse, then 25b–26a, 28, 12 ff. would yield an excellent sequence. Vv. 34–6 show traces of Luke's own vocabulary (προσέχετε ἑαυτοῖς, ἐπιστῇ, δεόμενοι), but there is no real ground for regarding them as purely editorial. V. 34, as we have seen, appears to go back to the same common tradition as I Thess. 5.3.

'Then he said to them, . . . They will lay their hands on you and persecute you, delivering you up to the synagogues and prisons, and you will be brought before kings and governors for my name's sake. This will be a time for you to bear testimony. Settle it therefore in your minds, not to meditate beforehand how to answer; for I will give you a mouth and wisdom, which none of your adversaries will be able to withstand or contradict. . . . And not a hair of your head will perish. By your endurance you will gain your lives.

'But when you see Jerusalem surrounded by armies, then know that its desolation has come near . . . And let those who are inside the city depart, and let not those who are out in the country enter it; for these are days of vengeance, to fulfil all that is written. . . . For great distress shall be upon the land[1] and wrath upon this people; they will fall by the edge of the sword, and be led captive among all nations; and Jerusalem will be trodden down by the Gentiles, until the times of the Gentiles are fulfilled . . . But when these things begin to take place, look up and raise your heads, because your redemption is drawing near . . .

'But take heed to yourselves lest your hearts be weighed down with dissipation and drunkenness and cares of this life, and that day come upon you suddenly like a snare; for it will come upon all who dwell upon the face of the whole land. But watch at all times praying that you may have strength to escape all these things that will take place, and to stand before the Son of man.'

Here again we have, not an apocalypse centring upon a *Parousia*, but a prophetic utterance giving warning of the things that must come upon the nation and a promise of deliverance out of them for those who are prepared and alert. It is to be noted how naturally the final injunctions, which we found Paul echoing with reference to the Day of the Lord, relate here to the day of Jerusalem's siege, and how the whole crisis is again interpreted, as we suggested earlier,[2] in terms of a judgement of the Son of man.[3]

---

[1] Both here and in v. 35 below the original reference of τῆς γῆς would appear to be to Judaea; but in the apocalypse as it now stands it must mean the whole earth, upon which the *Parousia* is to come simultaneously (cf. Luke 17.24 = Matt. 24.27).

[2] Pp. 77 f. above.

[3] A. Feuillet in his article 'Le sens du mot Parousie dans l'Evangile

Furthermore, if this was the original form and purpose of the eschatological discourse, into which the supra-historical climax of the *Parousia* has been inserted, it sets in a different light the warnings to watchfulness which in Mark, as in Luke, form its coda. The parable of the Fig-tree (Mark 13.28 f.) will refer, not to the imminence of the *Parousia,* but, quite naturally, to the suddenness with which the final attack upon the City will come:

'So also, when you see these things taking place, know that it is near, at the very gates.'

Whether this specific application was made by Jesus himself is here irrelevant. It points in any case to an application of the parable by the Church which has no reference as yet to the *Parousia*. Again, without vv. 24–7, the words about 'this generation' in v. 30 are no longer a prophecy about the end of the world and the return of Christ, but a straightforward historical judgement, comparable with the 'Q' saying of Matt. 23.36=Luke 11.51, that it is upon the present generation that the final judgement of the nation must fall. And it becomes possible that 'that day and that hour' may not after all have a supra-historical reference of any kind, whether to the *Parousia* or, as we argued, to the final 'day of the Lord', but allude to the same event as 'that day' in Luke 21.34, namely, the capture of the City. But the extremely solemn wording of 'not even the angels in heaven, nor the Son, but only the Father' suggest something more. In any case, whatever their original application for Jesus, this and the other sayings at the end of

---

de Matthieu' in *The Background of the New Testament and its Eschatology* (ed. W. D. Davies and D. Daube), pp. 261–80, also draws attention to the evidence for thinking that, prior to the Pauline *Parousia* doctrine, the reference of the eschatological discourse was to the fall of Jerusalem interpreted as the final judgement upon the Jewish nation. But he fails to carry conviction when he argues that this is what *Matthew* meant by the word *Parousia* or, in this discourse only, by 'the consummation of the age'.

Mark 13 can readily be seen as an appropriate tail-piece to a discourse that at one stage contained no reference to the *Parousia*.

A document of this kind, comprising teaching of Jesus collected and repointed for the purpose, would have circulated as a sort of broadsheet to provide guidance and warning to Christians in Palestine as the political situation came to a head. And it seems to have been in wide demand. Three versions of it, at any rate, have survived, in the Markan source (Mark 13), in 'Q' (Luke 17) and in the special Lucan material (Luke 21).[1] And, there may be the beginning of yet another in Luke 12 4–12, verses which reiterate many of the themes of Luke 21. 12–19. In this case, the parables of watchfulness which follow in 12.35–40 could have performed the same function as those at the end of the other discourses in Mark 13.28–37 and Luke 21.34 f. And, as the climax of *such* a document, the conclusion, 'You also must be ready; for the Son of man is coming at an hour you do not expect' (v. 40), would not have been a reference to the *Parousia* at all[2] but, like Luke 21.36, an exhortation to be prepared and able 'to stand[3] before the Son of man' in the judgement of 'all these things that will take place'. We should then be dealing with an intermediate stage in the history of the tradition. The parabolic warnings, that is to say, which were originally addressed to the Jews in Jesus' *life-time*,[4] came, by attachment to other teaching, to be applied to the Christian Church as a guide to the period *following his death*, the final

---

[1]We have already argued that Matt. 10.23 (from the special Matthean source) belonged originally to such a document and in John many elements of the same material reappear, as we shall see, in chapters 14–16.

[2]This verse, together, probably, with Luke 17.24, provides the only solid ground for supposing that the 'Q' material (if indeed it stood in 'Q'; cf. p. 79 n.3 above) was already applied to the *Parousia* prior to its incorporation in Matthew and Luke. It therefore begins to look as though it may in fact at this stage have had a different reference.

[3]I.e. not to be condemned like the rest; cf. Ps. 1.5; Mal. 3.2.

[4]As they still are in Luke 12.54–13.9.

stage being the transposition of all this teaching to provide a programme for *the end of the world.*

This last stage was effected by the fusion of such a flysheet as we have described with material from another of a rather different kind. This is the sort of which examples are to be found in II Thess. 2.1–12 and later in II Peter 3.3–10 and in the visions that compose the book of Revelation. Such compositions stand in the line, not of Amos, Isaiah and Jeremiah, but of Daniel, Enoch and IV Ezra. They also set out to be interpretations of coming events, but in terms of the esoteric, the mythological and the frankly supernatural. In contrast with the other type, they do not appear in origin to have been constructed from the teaching of Jesus at all—there is, as we have seen, singularly little trace of this either in II Thess. 2.1–12 or in Mark 13.24–7—but, according to the tradition of Jewish apocalyptic, out of the imagery of the Old Testament. The fusion of one type with the other was as easy, and probably as unnoticed, as the original passage from Prophecy to Apocalyptic. But the step was momentous.

By the incorporation of this material a new dimension and a new twist is given to the whole of the so-called eschatological discourse of the Gospels. It now becomes an apocalypse. Editorial touches transform the marks of time into a carefully graduated programme,[1] and, as we have seen, the introductory question is in due course adapted to its new content (Matt. 24.3). The transition from the original teaching of Jesus is therewith taken to the point at which the *Parousia* expectation meets us in Thessalonians. We are still no nearer to answering the question *why* that expectation arose—this must engage us in the next chapter—but we have gone some way in suggesting how it entered the Gospel tradition and describing the stages

[1]Thus, in Mark 13: v. 7, 'the end is not yet'; 8, 'this is but the beginning of the sufferings'; 10, 'the gospel must first be preached to all nations'; 14, 'then let those who are in Judaea flee to the mountains'; 21, 'and then if any one says to you . . .'; 24, 'after that tribulation'; 26, 'then they will see the Son of man . . .'; 27, 'and then he will send out the angels'.

involved. We have also narrowed the gap in time and located the decisive step nearer to the end than the beginning of the tunnel period.

Now, if the hypothesis that has been propounded is valid, another line of inquiry is opened up. We said earlier that, not only is Mark 13 as it stands dominated and governed in its interpretation by the paragraph on the *Parousia*, but the entire Markan conception of the consummation of Jesus' work is dominated and must be interpreted by chapter 13 thus understood. But if this chapter was *not* originally thus understood, what are the repercussions for the theology of the Gospel as a whole? Did Mark himself plan his Gospel under the influence of its existing apocalypse, or does it reveal a different, and earlier, conception of the climax to Jesus' work? We have already seen how the promise of the coming on the clouds as Jesus originally understood it, in the Trial saying of 14.62, and as the Evangelist must be interpreting it, in the light of 13.26, are very different. The question now is whether, *prior* to the introduction of 13.26, Mark, or the community behind him, did not perhaps view the consummation of Jesus' work in closer accord with Jesus' own understanding of it. If it could be concluded that the Gospel as a whole was planned originally with that rather than the later conception as its climax, we should then have a much broader picture of the stage in the Church's thinking that lay behind the *Parousia* doctrine.

Once again, such a conclusion cannot be demonstrated to the point of proof: it can only be shown to be a more or less probable hypothesis. But it should be emphasized that, if the *Parousia* conception of Mark 13.26 does represent an element secondary to the rest of the chapter, then it is just as much a hypothesis to say that it is *not* secondary to the rest of the Gospel as to affirm that it is. To maintain that it always coloured and determined the remainder of the Gospel, if the probability is that it did not colour and determine the remainder of the chapter, is a position that would need to be established with equally compelling evidence. Indeed, it is on this side that the burden of proof would lie.

But so accustomed are we, quite naturally, to reading the Gospel as a whole in the light of its existing climax that it requires a distinct effort to realize that there is in fact nothing in Mark apart from 13.26 that demands a culmination of the kind there described. The saying at the Trial, so far from requiring it, betrays by its very context that it was originally understood differently; and it is only 13.26 which would lead us to suppose that the Evangelist himself interpreted it in any other manner. The reference in 8.38 to the moment when the Son of man will come in the glory of his Father with the holy angels, is, as we have said, equally patient of either interpretation—as coming from heaven, in line with 13.26, or as a coming into glory, in line with 14.62.

These are the only sayings in Mark to speak of a coming in glory. The sole suggestion of a future coming in visitation is in the two parables of the Fig-tree and Porter in 13.28 f. and 33–7. But, as we have just seen, prior to the insertion of 13.24–7, these warnings would have referred, not to the *Parousia* at all, but to the fall of Jerusalem. And, at an earlier stage still, the latter parable, at any rate, almost certainly had the same setting as the only other parable of visitation which Mark records, that of the Wicked Husbandmen. This is remarkable for being the only parable of its kind to show no trace of application to a future coming nor any tendency towards apocalyptic, from which indeed all the Markan material, with the sole exception of 13.24–7, is, I believe, completely free.[1]

This will appear a surprising conclusion. But if it is true, it must tell heavily against the view that the theology of the

---

[1]There are, of course, the editorial touches already mentioned to bring chapter 13 as a whole into line with its present climax. The allusion in 13.14a to 'the abomination of desolation' betrays the same cast of mind as II Thess. 2.3 f. and has already been recognized as secondary. The reference to the coming in glory in 8.38, which we had reason to regard as secondary, may also have been added at the same stage as the introduction of 13.26.

Gospel as a whole was originally of a piece with the *Parousia* paragraph. Clearly it is *compatible* with it, and it has indeed been adjusted to it with reasonable skill. But the positive case for the alternative view rests upon showing that, without 13.24–7, the Gospel consistently presupposes a *different* conclusion, loose ends of which have not in fact been thoroughly tied into the present pattern of the whole.

Any reconstruction of the climax to which St Mark's Gospel points is rendered precarious by the uncertainty about its ending. With most scholars, I cannot believe that it was intended to stop at 16.8, where the best manuscripts terminate. But since in the reconstruction that follows I reach a conclusion very like that of the late Professor R. H. Lightfoot who believed firmly that this was the case,[1] it is evidently not a difference that need be decisive.

Lightfoot,[2] like Lohmeyer[3] before him, argued that the promise of Jesus to precede his disciples into Galilee implied a *Parousia* scene in Galilee as the culmination of the Markan story. In 16.7, 'It is there that you will see him, as he told you', has the same reference, they believed, as the prediction of seeing the Son of man in 13.26 and 14.62. Such an exegesis is bound to fail as an interpretation of Mark's intention as it now stands. For clearly the promise of 13.26 is not, as in 14.28, of a localized appearance to the inner circle of the disciples immediately after the Resurrection, but of a descent from heaven at the end of the world to gather the elect from every corner. Whatever climax may originally have been intended in Galilee has been superseded by an entirely different conception. But, *apart* from this passage, such an interpretation does, I believe, afford an entirely consistent picture of the theology of Mark.

According to the Trial saying, Jesus affirms as the climax to his ministry of suffering and death an immediate translation into the glory of his Father. This is to be the *Parousia* in its

---

[1] *Locality and Doctrine in the Gospels*, chapters I and II.
[2] Op. cit., pp. 61–5.
[3] *Galiläa und Jerusalem*, pp. 10–14; cf. Schweitzer, *The Quest of the Historical Jesus*, 3rd ed., p. 386 n. 1.

aspect of vindication, a coming to appear before the presence of God in exaltation and triumph—from then on. And it is of this that Jesus promises the disciples a vision in Galilee, 'after he is raised'. It is to be a visible confirmation, that is to say, not only that he is alive, but that he reigns thenceforth in all the power and splendour of God.[1]

Now in its present state the Gospel of Mark contains no such scene. But the first Gospel does. Matthew describes— and that as the direct fulfilment of the Galilee predictions (28. 7, 10, 16)—an appearing of Jesus to the disciples which is a *Parousia* scene in all but the name (28.16–20). It is, as Lightfoot says,[2] 'a manifestation of the Lord as possessing after the Resurrection all the attributes expected to be found in him at the *Parousia,* that is, above all, as the Son of man'.[3] But it is a picture, not of a descent in clouds at the end of the world, but of an exaltation in power with the promise of a presence *until* the end of the world. In it Jesus is seen and worshipped by the Eleven, elevated upon a mountain; and, coming to them, he says:

'All authority in heaven and on earth has been given to me; . . . and lo, I am with you always, to the close of the age.'

The insertion into this passage of the commission to baptize all nations in the name of the Trinity[4] has led to its being regarded as editorial and late. But as a climax to the Gospel it is so completely out of line with the rest of Matthew's eschatology

---

[1]So also A. M. Ramsey, 'What was the Ascension?' *Studiorum Novi Testamenti Societas,* Bulletin II, p. 49.

[2]Op. cit., p. 84; cf. the subsequent and very important treatment of this passage by Lohmeyer, 'Mir ist gegeben alle Gewalt', published posthumously in *In Memoriam Ernst Lohmeyer* (ed. W. Schmauch), pp. 22–49.

[3]With Matt. 28.18–20, cf. the description of the Son of man in Dan. 7.14: 'And to him was given dominion and glory and kingdom, that all peoples, nations, and languages should serve him; his dominion is an everlasting dominion, which shall not pass away'.

[4]Cf. Lohmeyer, op. cit., *In Memoriam Ernst Lohmeyer*, pp. 29 f.

that I cannot believe that he himself created it. As Dr Dodd has said, this is precisely the sort of ending that St Mark's Gospel requires;[1] and it is, I believe, the easiest assumption that it was from here in fact that Matthew derived it, before the text of Mark was mutilated.[2] In this case, the climax to which the theology of Mark points is the vision depicted in 14.62 rather than in 13.26. The Gospel, that is to say, looks forward, not to a coming again after an interval, but to an exaltation in glory, issuing in an abiding presence, from the Resurrection onwards. If this is so, it would provide additional reason for supposing that Mark 14.62 originally contained some such qualifying phrase as 'from now on'. And we can see too why it should subsequently have been omitted by the

[1] *The Interpretation of the Fourth Gospel*, p. 440. Such in fact is the conclusion that Lightfoot's own argument presupposes (cf. op. cit., p. 65). But for Lightfoot the Gospel *could* not have contained a description of it: for to Mark this event was the consummation itself, and that, as we know from 13.26, had still not occurred. But this follows only if the expectation of a *Parousia* in Galilee is interpreted in terms of the apocalyptic finality of 13.26. Lightfoot is understandably evasive (p. 44 n. 2) when pressed with the question whether Mark, writing in Rome 35 years later, was still looking for a climax in Galilee. Naturally, he was not: that had taken place, as described in Matt. 28.16–20. But since then an alternative conception of the *Parousia* had been superimposed upon it, and, at any rate in the present mutilated form of the Gospel, has now supplanted it. A deliberate suppression of the ending, as of the ἀπ᾽ ἄρτι in 14.62, cannot indeed be ruled out.

[2] It is impossible to tell whether Luke knew of this ending. For he has obliterated all references to such a culmination in Galilee (cf. Luke 24.6 with Mark 16.7), as evidently inconsistent with the later *Parousia* doctrine, just as he has omitted from the Trial saying the promise of an immediate coming on the clouds. But he is probably aware of the tradition which connected a coming on the clouds with a scene of *exaltation*. For in his Ascension narrative he appears to be trying to harmonize this earlier conception with its subsequent understanding as a descent: 'Men of Galilee [*sic*], why do you stand looking into heaven? This Jesus, who was taken up from you into heaven, will come in the same way as you saw him go into heaven' (Acts 1.11; cf. the deliberate (?) parallelism between '*a* cloud' in Luke 21.27 and Acts 1.9).

Church which used his Gospel; for the eschatology of which this saying formed part had since been revised.

Support for this reconstruction of the Markan purpose may be found in the narrative of the Transfiguration. In his valuable monograph, *St Mark and the Transfiguration Story*, Dr G. H. Boobyer has argued that the Transfiguration is to be understood, and was understood by Mark, as an anticipation of the *Parousia*.[1] But, if this is true, as I believe it is, then it is clearly of a *Parousia* viewed primarily in terms not of visitation but of vindication, just as, in II Peter 1.16–18, the guarantee of 'the power and *parousia* of our Lord Jesus Christ' is provided by the moment on the mountain 'when he received honour and glory from God the Father'. For the evidence Dr Boobyer assembles points even more strongly to a conclusion which he does not draw, namely, that the *Parousia* vision was originally conceived in terms of exaltation and ascent. It is to such an investiture with glory that the Transfiguration points forward.

This interpretation is borne out by features in the other traditions. According to the Lucan account, Moses and Elijah, who appear in glory, speak with Jesus of 'the departure which he was to accomplish at Jerusalem' (9.31); and Professor H. J. Cadbury is, I believe, right in taking the allusion to be to their own experiences of assumption which Jesus is to share,[2] and for which, a few verses later (9.51), he sets his face to go to Jerusalem, 'when the days were accomplished for him *to be received up*'. In the second century *Apocalypse of Peter* the Transfiguration story is in fact fused with an account of the Ascension, whose glory it anticipates, and Jesus, Moses and Elijah are borne away to heaven on a cloud.[3] The same tradition may be reflected in the strange incident in Rev. 11.1–13 of

---

[1] I Peter, which I believe to come from the same place and date, also witnesses to this understanding, if 'a partaker in the glory that is to be revealed' (5.1) refers (as II Peter 1.16–18 evidently refers it) to the Transfiguration. *Vide* E. G. Selwyn, *I Peter*, ad loc.

[2] 'Acts and Eschatology', *The Background of the New Testament and its Eschatology* (ed. W. D. Davies and D. Daube), p. 309.

[3] M. R. James, *The Apocryphal New Testament*, pp. 518 f.

the two witnesses (clearly, I believe, intended as Moses and Elijah), whose vindication out of terrible humiliation and death is proclaimed by a 'voice from heaven saying to them, "Come up hither!"'. And in the sight of their foes they went up to heaven in a cloud'.

In all this, the symbolism of the language of the clouds is the same as in the scene of Dan. 7.13, and it is such a crowning glory of the Son of man that the vision on the mountain prefigures. As Mark evidently intended by his connexion between 8.38 and 9.1 and 2, the Transfiguration is to be seen as anticipating the moment when the Son of man and the kingdom of God shall have come with power. Following immediately the prediction of his rising again out of humiliation and death, it points to a climax of the work of Jesus conceived in terms of an entry through suffering into the triumph of God. 'Was it not necessary that the Christ should suffer these things and (so) enter into his glory?' (Luke 24.26): no words could summarize better the crucial section of Mark's narrative from 8.29 to 9.13, and indeed the movement of his Gospel as a whole. For such is the insistent conclusion to which, the paragraph of 13.24–7 apart, his entire eschatology points.

And, even in Luke, it should be observed that these words are spoken on Easter Day itself. Already the King, returning to his own, has entered upon his reign. Except in Acts 1.1–11, there is no trace within the New Testament—or for some time outside it—of an interval between the Resurrection and Ascension. There is but a single movement of exaltation by and to the right hand of God (Acts 2.33 f.; 5.31; Phil. 2.9 f.; I Peter 1.21). Even in Acts 1.1–11, Père Benoit has argued,[1] the departure of Jesus from the disciples' sight is not depicted by Luke as the real moment of his glorification. To be sure Luke is not unambiguous at this point; for in Acts 1 he has identified the moment when the appearances ceased (to which Paul also witnesses by describing his own appearance as 'to

---

[1] R. P. P. Benoit, 'L'Ascension', *Revue Biblique* LVI (1949), pp. 198–200; cf. A. N. Wilder, 'Variant Traditions of the Resurrection in Acts,' *Journal of Biblical Literature*, LXII (1943), pp. 307–18.

one *untimely* born' (I Cor. 15.8)) with the 'ascension' of Jesus, which elsewhere he associates with his death and resurrection.[1] But even while Luke places the physical return of Jesus to the Father after forty days, his account of it lacks any signs that this, to use the Johannine phrase, is intended as 'the hour when the Son of man is glorified'. Apart from the cloud, whose function, as the angels indicate in 1.11, is to establish the link with the later *Parousia,* there is a complete absence of any language of theophany such as Luke associates both with the Baptism (3.21 f.) and the Transfiguration (9.28–36). What the story marks is the final withdrawal of the Christ who has *already* been exalted to the Father's side but who has returned for a limited period to show himself to his disciples. Just as the appearances are proofs that Jesus is *already* alive, so what is afforded to the disciples is confirmation that the Ascension is even now a reality, that Jesus is 'from now on . . . seated at the right hand of the power of God' (Luke 22.69), that he has 'come into his kingdom' (23.42 f.) and 'entered his glory' (24.26). Equally, in Matthew, the vision of Jesus granted to the Eleven is to show that 'all authority in heaven and on earth has been given' to him (28.18); and, in John 20.19–23, the bestowal of the Spirit on the disciples is the sure sign that Jesus has already been 'glorified' (cf. John 7.39), that he has by now ascended to the Father (cf. John 20.17).

The distinction between the Resurrection and Ascension is not one of time but of theological emphasis. In the earliest tradition, the vision that he is alive and the vision that he is sovereign are one and the same. It is only later that the two elements come to be treated separately. The primitive witness was that Jesus was 'designated Son of God in power' (the

[1] I take the shorter text of Luke 24.51 f. to be original and to describe a simple parting of Jesus from the disciples. The additional words, 'and he was carried up into heaven' and 'they worshipped him', appear to be a clumsy attempt to equate 'termination of appearances' with 'ascension', as in Acts 1, despite the fact that the Ascension is then made to occur on Easter day. For Luke, we shall argue, the real exaltation of Jesus *did* take place on Easter day, but *before* the appearances.

essential message of the Ascension) 'by (*or* from) his resurrection from the dead' (Rom. 1.4); and this, as M. Goguel argued, would point to a manifestation of Jesus in glory at the time of the Resurrection declaring him to be Son of God, precisely such as is anticipated in the Transfiguration vision.[1]

In the same way, there was, I believe, in origin no interval between the Exaltation of Jesus so conceived and his *Parousia*. The difference, again, was not one of temporal sequence but of theological emphasis. To describe the glorification of Christ in terms of *Parousia* is to fix attention not so much upon the crowning of the previous humiliation as upon the release thenceforward of the sovereignty thus inaugurated. The vision of the *Parousia* is the vision of the Son of man, not only as seated at the right hand of God, but as coming in his power. But, whether viewed as Exaltation or as *Parousia*, the conception is in each case of a sovereignty inaugurated from then on, though only inaugurated. The witness of the vision is, strictly, 'a *partaker* in the glory that *is to be* revealed' (I Peter 5.1).

To sum up, the climax to the ministry of Jesus, as the primitive tradition conceived it, is his receiving up into the presence and triumph of God, from which, already glorified, he shows himself to the disciples,[2] and from which henceforth he

---

[1] *Jean Baptiste*, pp. 218–20. Cf. the organic interrelation between the anticipation and its fulfilment implied by the words, 'He charged them to tell no man what they had seen, until the Son of man should have risen from the dead' (Mark 9.9), and by the recurrence in each scene in Luke of the 'two men' (Luke 9.30; 24.4; Acts 1.10).

[2] If Benoit is correct in his interpretation of the Lucan Ascension narrative as the moment rather of adieu than of glorification, then all our witnesses testify to the Resurrection appearances as lying *the other side* of the exaltation of Christ. Paul allows no distinction between his own vision of the Lord in glory and those granted to the others (I Cor. 15.5–8). Matthew 28.16–20, as we have seen, describes an appearance of Jesus in heavenly splendour; and John 20.17–28 implies that the glorification and ascension of Jesus to the Father takes place before complete union with the disciples is re-established. The view that the appearances were of the exalted Christ does not therefore of itself argue (if Luke and John are

pours out his Spirit on the Church and comes to his world in judgement and power. From now on the future belongs to Christ—till the final consummation of this age and the reduction of its powers to the authority he has been given. Of this future the immediate sequel can even now be glimpsed (Mark 13.5–23; etc.): indeed, it is written already in letters of blood, the blood which remains to be required of that fateful generation (Matt. 23.35 f.=Luke 11.50 f.; Mark 13.30; Luke 23.28–31). And this catastrophic climax is seen and interpreted as an integral part of the coming of the Son of man begun already in the ministry of Jesus (Luke 21.36; cf. Matt. 10.23; Luke 18.8).

But of some second eschatological moment, of another advent of Christ after an interval—of this we saw no evidence in the teaching of Jesus; of it too we found no signs in the earliest preaching and creeds of the Church; and now, unless our argument be completely mistaken, there would appear to be a stage of development in the Gospel tradition from which it is equally absent. As this stage includes the whole of Mark up to its latest recension, the very important special Lucan source (which contains no certain reference to the *Parousia*) and possibly 'Q',[1] it is clearly of far-reaching significance, and takes us well on into the period of the Church's thinking.

---

witnesses to it) that they must have been conceived as purely visionary, let alone that the exaltation was regarded as taking place directly from the Cross and that the idea of resurrection from a tomb is a later materialization (as G. Bertram supposes in his article, 'Die Himmelfahrt Jesus vom Kreuz aus und der Glaube an seine Auferstehung', *Festgabe für Adolf Deissmann*, pp. 187–217). Cf. Benoit, op. cit., pp. 197 f.; Boobyer, op. cit., pp. 24 f.; P. Menoud, 'Remarques sur les textes de l'ascension dans Luc-Actes', *Neutestamentliche Studien für R. Bultmann* (ed. W. Eltester), pp. 148 f.

[1] Cf. p. 126 n. 2 above. The special Matthean source, in contrast to the editorial work of Matthew, has at most a single reference to the *Parousia*, that in Matt. 10.23 ('You will not have gone through all the towns of Israel, before the Son of man comes'), and this we have argued belonged originally to the same pre-*Parousia* stratum as the bulk of Mark 13.

Indeed, with the exception perhaps of the 'Q' material, one could say that, within the Gospels, the application of the teaching of Jesus to a *Parousia* after an interval is a purely editorial feature. It cannot be demonstrated to have moulded the tradition prior to the work of the Evangelists themselves. And even the Evangelists are not completely united on this. John, we shall maintain in the final chapter, is witness to a tradition quite unaffected by it. It is to be detected only in the final editing (or should one say, subsequent recension?) of Mark—though this was to prove decisive, through its influence upon Matthew and Luke. Of these two, however, it is only Matthew who carries the process further, which he does at almost every opportunity. Luke takes over the idea of a final *Parousia* and includes it in his line of salvation events: the life and death of Jesus, the resurrection, the appearances, the ascension, the giving of the Spirit, the evangelism of the world, and, finally, the coming in glory. But he does not dilate upon it. Nowhere does he create a *Parousia* saying from one that previously contained no reference to it, and at one important point (22.69) he suppresses a mention of it. In Acts, likewise, there is no explicit reference to the *Parousia* once the framework of events is fixed in 1.11, though Luke himself must have understood the promise of 3.20 f. to apply to it, whatever (as we shall argue in the next chapter) was its meaning for his original source.

But, though the influence of the *Parousia* idea cannot be demonstrated with certainty till a relatively late stage in the tradition, this may always be said to be due to the scantiness of our evidence. And indeed the argument from silence would again be precarious, were it not for the complementary fact that in each of the cases we have examined—the original teaching of Jesus; the first apostolic preaching; the primitive creeds; and the earliest state of the Gospel tradition—there are always the marks of a single, self-consistent alternative, from which mention of a subsequent *Parousia* shows no sign of having been accidentally or fortuitously omitted. This alternative consists in a fully inaugurated eschatology, according to which, from the Resurrection onwards, the Christ comes in power to his own, till all is finally subjected to that saving sovereignty which God has willed to accomplish through him.

But if indeed this was the earliest theology, not only of Jesus, but of the Church as well, why was it broken up? Why was the eschatological event divided into two acts? Why did the Christ come to be expected twice?

WHY WAS CHRIST EXPECTED
TWICE?

In the previous chapters we have tried to determine by what process and at what stage the *Parousia* belief entered the thinking of the Church and became grafted on to the tradition of the teaching of Jesus. But its actual origin remains undetermined. If it did not derive from the teaching of Jesus, from where did it come?

There are in fact two questions involved here. The first concerns the source of the language. How was it that the Church came to depict the kind of scene such as is described in Thessalonians and reflected with variations throughout the New Testament from Mark 13 to II Peter and the Apocalypse?

It was to this question that Dr T. F. Glasson addressed himself in his book, *The Second Advent*. Having demonstrated that the expectation of a descent of the Christ in glory from heaven formed no part of the Jewish hope, he proceeded to show with a wealth of illustration (pp. 162–79) how the language in which the *Parousia* expectation is couched derives, not from *messianic* passages of the Old Testament, but from its visions of the coming of *God* to his people in final and glorious theophany. 'Broadly speaking', he wrote, 'the Christians took over the Old Testament doctrine of the Advent of the Lord, making the single adjustment that the Lord was the Lord Jesus' (p. 176). This conclusion is in line with the use of the term *parousia* itself, which in Judaism is never in any certain passage employed of the Messiah but, about this time, was being applied to the appearance of God[1] or of the day of God.[2] From a careful study of the term Professor G. D. Kilpatrick draws the inference that 'the use of *parousia* in Christian writings from St Paul onward is a theological development of the same kind as the use of *kyrios* (Lord) as a title for Jesus'.[3]

This explanation of the origin of the *Parousia* language requires only one qualification. It accounts fully for the evidence of the Epistles, where 'the Lord' is the regular title for the expected Jesus. But in the Gospels, except in one instance, 'Watch therefore, for you do not know on what day *your Lord* is coming' (Matt. 24.42), where the vocabulary is taken from the parable behind it (Mark 13.35), it is not *as Lord* that Jesus is expected to come, but as Son of man (e.g., Matt. 24.44=Luke 12.40). Indeed, in the only other combination of these terms, 'I tell you, you will not see me again, until you say, "Blessed be he who *comes* in the name of *the Lord*" ' (which forms, for Matthew (23.39), a direct lead into the *Parousia* discourse), 'the Lord' is not Jesus but God.

The Church's language about the *Parousia* must therefore be derived, not merely from the Old Testament theophanies, but from the mouth of Jesus himself. It is, I believe, inexplicable unless he did speak of a 'coming of the Son of man', though we have argued that on his lips the phrase had a very different reference, namely, to the visitation of God to his people focused in the challenge and climax of his own ministry.

But even when the source of the *language* is accounted for, there is still a second and deeper question. Once the idea of a second coming has arisen, it is natural that it should receive

[1] E.g., Test. Jud. 22.2; Josephus, *Antt.* III v. 2; cf. II Enoch 32.1, which speaks of God's 'second coming' after his first visitation at creation (58.1).

[2] II Baruch 55.6; cf. II Pet. 3.12.

[3] 'Acts 7.52, ἔλευσις', *Journal of Theological Studies*, XLVI (1945), pp. 136–45. Cf. J. Dupont, op. cit., pp. 49–64; B. Rigaux, op. cit., pp. 196–201; M. Dibelius' note on παρουσία at I Thess. 2.20 in Lietzmann's *Handbuch zum N.T.*; A. Oepke in Kittel, *T.W.N.T.*, V, pp. 861–3.

embodiment and embellishment from the classic descriptions of the final glory of God. But whence the very notion of a double advent? Above all, why should there be two comings *of the Christ?* That Jewish expectations of the End which were focused upon the appearance of some messianic figure and those which looked rather to a direct intervention by God himself should have coalesced into a coming of the Christ followed by a final advent of God would be understandable enough.[1] That the Christ should come some considerable time before the final day of the Lord was again an idea that had roots in Judaism.[2] Even the expectation of two messianic figures, representing between them the priestly and royal functions of 'the Lord's Anointed', is now indicated by the Dead Sea Scrolls.[3] What is entirely unprecedented is the notion of two separate comings of the Christ. Nowhere in Judaism is there any such conception, and it is this that cries for explanation.

The explanation, I believe, is to be sought in an unresolved crisis in the Christology of the primitive Church, centring in the problem whether or not the messianic event had yet taken place, whether *the Christ* had come or not. The solution, as so often, was a compromise: part of it had taken place and part of it had not, the Christ had come and yet would come. Hence the idea of the messianic drama in two acts separated by an interval. Such, at any rate, is the thesis which will be argued in what follows. It cannot be more than a hypothesis. And even

[1] A similar process in fact overtook the expectation of the return of Elijah. The promise of Mal. 4.5, that Elijah would come before the great and terrible day of *the Lord*, became assimilated to the other and parallel expectation of the coming of the Messiah. As a result, in Christianity, aided by its description of Jesus as 'the Lord', Elijah becomes the forerunner not of God but of the Christ, who then himself comes before the final day of God.

[2] E.g., IV Ezra 7.28 f. For the other evidence, *vide* J. W. Bailey, 'The Temporary Messianic Reign in the Literature of Early Judaism', *Journal of Biblical Literature*, LIII (1934), pp. 170–87.

[3] *Manual of Discipline* (1QS) ix, 11; cf. 1QSa ii, 11–22. Cf. K. G. Kuhn, 'Die beiden Messias Aarons und Israels', *New Testament Studies*, I (1955), pp. 168–79.

if it is not wholly adequate, the facts of the problem remain until some better hypothesis is forthcoming.

It will be recalled that at the end of the first chapter we found in the primitive preaching, as it is recorded in the early sermons of Acts, no reference to a return or future coming of Christ. This preaching ends on the note that Jesus, vindicated by God as Lord and Christ from the moment of the Resurrection, reigns henceforth till all his foes submit, and that in the Spirit he has poured forth the power by which this is to be accomplished. This reign has yet indeed to reach its consummation in the final day of the Lord and in the judgement to which, already, Jesus has been appointed by God. But there is no hint of a second messianic event in history and no idea of the Christ coming again. This position we shall refer to in future as that of Acts 2, since this is the chapter in which it receives its most complete statement.[1] But it is the position reflected generally in the other preaching summaries and confessional formulae and represents the established gospel of the primitive Church.

But we noted that there was one exception to this consensus, which we reserved for later treatment; and this must now be examined. It is the speech attributed to Peter in Acts 3.

That section of it which sets out the gospel (vv. 13–15, 17–26) runs as follows:

'The God of Abraham and of Isaac and of Jacob, the God of our fathers, glorified his servant Jesus, whom you delivered up and denied in the presence of Pilate, when he had decided to release him. But you denied the Holy and Righteous One, and asked for a murderer to be granted to you, and killed the Author of life, whom God raised from the dead. To this we are witnesses. . . .

'And now, brethren, I know that you acted in ignorance, as did also your rulers. But what God foretold by the mouth of all the prophets, that his Christ should suffer, he thus fulfilled. Repent therefore, and turn again, that your sins may be blotted out, that times of refreshing may come from the presence of the Lord, and

[1]Only the reference to the judgement of Christ is absent, which occurs in Acts 10.42; cf. 17.31.

that he may send the Christ appointed for you, Jesus, whom heaven must receive until the time for establishing all that God spoke by the mouth of his holy prophets from of old. Moses said, "The Lord God will raise up for you a prophet from your brethren as he raised me up. You shall listen to him in whatever he tells you. And it shall be that every soul that does not listen to that prophet shall be destroyed from the people." And all the prophets who have spoken, from Samuel and those who came afterwards, also proclaimed these days. You are the sons of the prophets and of the covenant which God gave to your fathers, saying to Abraham, "And in your posterity shall all the families of the earth be blessed." God, having raised up his servant, sent him to you first, to bless you in turning every one of you from your wickedness.'

At first sight this speech contains a clear allusion to the *Parousia*. But the more closely it is examined, the less probable does it seem that this is in fact the reference. There is no statement here that the Christ is to return. The conception, rather, appears to be this:—Jesus has been sent by God as servant and prophet, in fulfilment of the prediction that God would raise up for his people a prophet like Moses. The purpose of this visitation was to bring the blessing covenanted to Abraham and an opportunity of repentance to Israel. Instead, the Jews have denied and killed God's servant. But even this has been within his plan: indeed, it has actually fulfilled it. He has not been defeated, but has exalted Jesus to his own splendour in heaven, where he must remain till the final day of restoration. Meanwhile, because the Jews and their leaders have acted in ignorance, opportunity for repentance is still open.[1] This they are urged to seize, that the age of renewal may dawn and God may be able to send Jesus, this time as their appointed Messiah.

According to this conception, Jesus is still only the Christ-elect; the messianic age has yet to be inaugurated. If we put the question, 'Art thou "he that should come", or are we to look for another?', the answer given here is: 'Yes, Jesus *is* the

[1]This is evidence of the primitive setting of the speech. Contrast the tone even of I Thess. 2.15 f.

one who shall come. We know who the Messiah will be; there is no need to look for another. The Messiah, to be sure, is still to come. But Jesus has already been sent, as the forerunner of the Christ he is to be, in the promised rôle of Servant and Prophet, with the offer of the covenanted blessing and a preaching of repentance. Accept that therefore, despite all that you have done, that you may be able to receive him in due time as the Christ, the bringer of God's new age'.

What are we to make of such a message and such a Christology?

Is it, in the first place, in fact a correct reconstruction of the passage? It has not normally been interpreted in this way.[1] This is partly because the later *Parousia* doctrine of the *return* of the Christ has almost inevitably been read into it. But there is also an element in the speech itself which militates against what otherwise seems to be its clear tenor. In v. 18 Peter is made to say: 'But what God announced beforehand through the mouth of all the prophets, that his Christ should suffer, he thus fulfilled'. That Jesus suffered *as the Christ* is clearly incompatible with the idea that he is still, even after the Resurrection, only the Christ-elect.

Were we compelled to accept the words 'that his Christ should suffer' as an integral part of the original speech, then it would be difficult on any reconstruction to find in it a consistent theology.[2] But there are strong indications that this is in fact an exegetical interpolation by Luke himself into the source that he is using.

In the first place, the idea of the *suffering* of Jesus plays no part in any other formulation of the primitive preaching. Not only is it not to be found in any of the speeches in Acts (where the betrayal, denial, crucifixion, death and burial of Jesus are

---

[1]For all details and references I must be allowed to refer to my article, 'The Most Primitive Christology of all?' in *The Journal of Theological Studies,* N.S., VII (1956), pp. 177–89, from which a number of paragraphs have here been taken.

[2]K. Lake and H. J. Cadbury, *The Beginnings of Christianity,* IV, p. 37, regard this verse as evidence that the speech is not authentic.

all mentioned), but it is also absent from the Pauline summaries, notably from that in I Cor. 15.3 f. where the Apostle speaks of Christ as having died for our sins, been buried, and raised on the third day.

Secondly, the thesis that *the Christ* (as distinct from the Son of man) should suffer is found on inspection to be a characteristic, and indeed peculiar, feature of Luke's writings. It occurs only in the Lucan summaries of the meaning of the ministry and death of Jesus placed in the mouth of the risen Lord and of Paul. In four such passages he declares that the whole message of the Prophets is to be found in the mystery that *the Christ* should suffer.[1] It would hardly be surprising then should he have introduced the phrase again into this speech in parenthetic exegesis of what was foretold by all the Prophets. The supposition that we have here an editorial interpolation is further strengthened by the fact that there is a similar interjection in Luke 17.25, 'But first he must suffer many things and be rejected of this generation', which we have already (p. 73) had reason to regard as a Lucan insertion.

We may, therefore, with reasonable confidence detach the phrase about the suffering of the Christ from the main body of the speech in Acts 3. Consciously or unconsciously, Luke is bringing this primitive summary with its heterodox theology into line with his own Christology. In so doing, he is in fact going beyond anything found in the rest of the early preaching, even in Acts 2, which asserts that Jesus is the Christ *by virtue of the Resurrection*.

The position of Acts 2 was not, of course, one at which the Church could stop. The recognition was soon to follow that at the Resurrection Jesus was merely designated 'with power'

---

[1] Luke 24.26 f. and 45 f.; Acts 17.2 f.; 26.22 f. In each of these instances, as in Acts 3.18, it is clear that ὁ χριστός is a *title*, and not simply a proper name as it is in I Peter, where the sufferings of Christ play a prominent rôle (a reason for which has been suggested by F. L. Cross, *I Peter: A Paschal Liturgy*, p. 14). The Lucan mystery is precisely that it is *as the Messiah* that Jesus should have suffered.

what eternally he was (Rom. 1.4), and his pre-existence is explicitly recognized in Phil. 2.6,[1] as the equivalent in Greek terms of his 'foreordination' (Acts 3.20). The next stage is the growing acknowledgement that what he was declared to be at the Resurrection must also have been valid (at least proleptically) even of his humiliation. By the time of St Mark's Gospel, at any rate, the whole public ministry is viewed as messianic (though it is still recognized that 'the Christ' is a title Jesus himself preferred to avoid). Finally, in Matthew and Luke, the application of 'Christ' and 'Lord' is pushed back, not merely behind the Resurrection, but behind the Baptism, to the birth of Jesus, so that there is no gap, no moment when, to quote the angel's words to the shepherds (Luke 2.11), 'Christ the Lord' is not the appropriate designation.[2]

The suggestion here being made is that this process did not begin with the position of Acts 2. Acts 3, I believe, represents a still more primitive stage, in which Jesus is not yet the Christ *even at the Resurrection:* the messianic event is still awaited. The demonstration that Acts 3 *is* more primitive, or, perhaps we should say, represents an alternative response within the Church to the meaning of Jesus that never developed beyond the primitive stage, rests upon a detailed linguistic comparison which would distract from our present argument.[3] In fact, it

[1]Both of these passages are widely taken to be pre-Pauline. *Vide,* most recently, E. Schweizer, *Erniedrigung und Erhöhung bei Jesus und seinen Nachfolgern,* pp. 52, 55 f.

[2]I owe to Professor John Knox (*Christ the Lord,* pp. 89–104) the recognition that this process of 'pushing back' the Church's Christology prior to the Resurrection did not follow a straight line, with pre-existence as the last stage (following the acknowledgment of Jesus as Son of God from birth), as one could conclude from placing the Fourth Gospel next in the sequence after Matthew and Luke. But this ignores the evidence of Paul. Rather, pre-existence came first (Knox detects it also in Mark); and the gap is then gradually closed during which it was originally thought incredible that Jesus could be acting *as the Messiah.* That he is distinctively the Christ when he suffers is, as we have seen, emphasized in the Gospels by Luke alone.

[3]*Vide* op. cit., *J.T.S.,* N.S., VII, pp. 185–7.

can, I believe, be shown that, whereas Acts 2 comes to us the
most finished and polished specimen of the established
Apostolic preaching, placed, as it were, in the shop window of
the Jerusalem Church and of Luke's narrative, Acts 3 (and to
some extent also Stephen's speech in Acts 7) preserves a
presentation, and in many cases a terminology, which was
destined to have no future in the Church's proclamation.[1]

But here we are concerned with this speech of Acts 3 only
as evidence for what we called earlier the unresolved crisis in
the Christology of the early Church.

From the beginning, we may presume, the whole Church
was faced, like the Baptist, with the all-decisive question of
whether Jesus was in fact 'the one who should come'. Any

[1]If this investigation were being pursued for its own sake, it
would be important to try and place this theology and its setting in
the life of the primitive Church. Here it is only possible to indicate
in briefest summary the direction in which I consider the answer to
lie. The thinking belongs, I believe, to those groups for whom the
question, 'Art thou he that should come?' must from the first have
been most pressing, those, namely, who entered the Church from
the following of John the Baptist. Hints of this are to be seen, for
instance, (a) in the understanding of Jesus as fulfilling the function,
not only of the Prophet like Moses, but also of Elijah, which lies
behind Acts 3.19–21 (*vide J.T.S.*, op. cit., p. 182), and corresponds
with John's expectation of the Coming One in terms of Mal. 3–4;
and (b) in the fact that for this way of thinking the final outpouring
of the Spirit, like the dawning of the messianic age, was apparently
still awaited (*vide* p. 153 below), a position associated in Acts 19.1–4
with (Christian) disciples who, admitting only the baptism of John,
evidently doubted whether the Mighty One, upon whose coming the
baptism of the Spirit depended (Mark 1.7 and pars), had yet come.
Thanks to the evidence of the Dead Sea Scrolls, it looks as if it
may be possible to relate these circles also to 'the Hellenists' (which
would explain the affinities with Stephen's speech), to Samaritan
groups, and to the Fourth Gospel. *Vide* O. Cullmann, 'The Significance of the Qumran Texts for Research into the Beginnings of
Christianity', *Journal of Biblical Literature*, LXXIV (1955), pp.
213–26; R. Gyllenburg, 'Die Anfänge der johanneischen Tradition'
in *Neutestamentliche Studien für R. Bultmann* (ed. W. Eltester),
pp. 144–7.

confidence the disciples may have acquired in the midst of his ministry and mighty works (cf. Matt. 11.2–6; Luke 7.18–23) must have been shattered by the Crucifixion; and the mood expressed in the words, 'But we had hoped that he was the one to redeem Israel' (Luke 24.21), was no doubt representative. The incredible reversal of the Resurrection re-opened the question. But it is facile to assume that it answered it at once.

During his life-time Jesus' followers had become accustomed to one who spoke of himself as God's servant-Son and also as the Son of man, whose full and glorious vindication to that heavenly office waited, however, upon the coming of God's Kingdom in power.[1] He had come in filial obedience as the Servant of the Lord to inaugurate God's mighty act, but always in his teaching the climax lay beyond his present humiliation and death. What the Father was to accomplish through him would indeed be recognized as the messianic act, but the title of Christ he declined to anticipate.[2] Those among whom he stood would see the Kingdom come with power and see himself, as Son of man, vindicated in the might and right of God; but to the end of the Ministry, even at the Last Supper itself (Mark 14.25; Luke 22.16–18), he was still looking forward and beyond.

We may be sure that the Resurrection restored, and immeasurably deepened, the conviction that Jesus could not have been mistaken. He was, beyond doubt, 'he that should come'. But it is entirely credible that the Resurrection should not at first have appeared so completely to alter the frame of reference that the decisive event was now to be seen, no longer in the future, however imminent, but in the past. Jesus *was* indeed the Coming One, the Christ to be: God had set his seal upon that. But to assert that, by virtue of the Resurrection, he was

[1] Cf. Fuller, op. cit., chapter IV.
[2] Cf. Schweitzer, *The Mystery of the Kingdom of God*, p. 211: 'How is it conceivable that the disciples proclaimed that Jesus had entered upon his messianic existence through the Resurrection, if already upon earth he had spoken of his messiahship as a dignity then actually possessed?'

already the Christ, that the messianic act, the eschatological event, *had now taken place*—that was a tremendous leap and required a second major adjustment. Nothing is more natural than that the first Christology should have expressed the Gospel within the same frame of reference in which Jesus himself preached it[1]—namely, that he had come among men as Servant of the Lord and as Prophet of the End, bringing the good news of the Kingdom and the final call to repentance, but that all this was but in preparation for the act which would inaugurate the messianic rule of God and vindicate him as the Christ. Indeed, if we had not such a theology as that which we have argued is represented in Acts 3, we should almost be compelled to supply it.

The full Christian gospel of God's act in Jesus waited indeed upon the recognition that the framework within which Jesus himself proclaimed the good news had itself been shattered by his own action. The Cross-and-Resurrection, incredible as it might seem, *was* the eschatological event of which Jesus had spoken so often to deaf ears. This was the redemptive act, and Jesus was even now the Christ and all else of which prophecy spoke. *From now on* the Messiah reigned at God's right hand and the age of fulfilment had been inaugurated.

Such is the proclamation of Acts 2 and the settled gospel of the Jerusalem Church. But the question remains whether in fact the Church ever resolved the hesitation reflected in Acts 3 with quite the decisiveness that Acts 2 suggests. Was it able to affirm the exaltation of Jesus as the messianic event, and therefore as the eschatological event, without remainder?

Even to raise the question is to give the answer. For Jesus himself, if our reconstruction has been correct, the climax of his own obedience in vindication out of death was the event

[1]Cf. Dodd, *The Parables of the Kingdom*, p. 133: 'When the apostles first made their proclamation, within a few weeks of the death of their Master, they may still have had the sense of living within the crisis, as they had lived during his brief ministry, though at a more advanced stage in it'.

through which God was to initiate the new covenant and introduce the messianic age. He looked, of course, to the final consummation of that age in a crowning judgement of God, in which he would share; but he did not look, as far as we can tell, to a second act in history after an interval, a 'part two' of his coming, incorporating elements, whether of vindication or of visitation, not introduced by the first.

The turning of the Church to wait for a second coming, appears to arise directly from the hesitation whether *this* piece of history *could*, fully, be called the messianic or eschatological event—not, of course, the End, in the sense of the last thing to happen, but the event that introduces into the world that by which God's purpose for it is finally declared and by which ultimately it must be saved and judged. That there was still a 'last day' in which all would be consummated no one thought of doubting. The hesitation was whether, within history, everything had now been inaugurated which that day would crown, or whether there were elements yet to enter it, another 'coming' *before* which the '*consummatum*' could not be declared. And that hesitation was never overcome. What of those aspects of the promised messianic rule which seemed to find no fulfilment in Jesus under the form of a servant? As in the Old Testament, unfulfilled prophecy was to prove the father of apocalyptic: features in the traditional picture of God's coming to reign, combined with those in Jesus' own teaching which did not yet appear to have been accounted for, materialized into a second, mythological event still to be awaited.

An illustration of this, derived from the material we have been considering, is the way in which in Acts 2.17–21 *all* the traditional imagery of the last times, not only of the outpouring of the Spirit, but of the signs in the earth and the sky, the sun and the moon, is applied to the event which marks the beginning of the new age and is seen as inaugurated in the miraculous phenomena of Pentecost. But later these 'signs', in themselves but a poetic way of describing the event as eschatological, are separated from the outpouring of the Spirit (which is regarded as fulfilled) to become the materials of another, purely supernatural occurrence, for which the Church still waits, when

'The sun will be darkened, and the moon will not give its light, and the stars will be falling from heaven, and the powers in the heavens will be shaken; and . . . they will see the Son of man coming in clouds' (Mark 13.24–6).

In the emergence of this second focus of Christian hope lies perhaps the abiding significance of Acts 3. As a Christological formulation it represents no more than a fossil, a residual survival of purely historical interest; for the Church was never to go back on its conviction that Jesus was now already, and indeed had been eternally, the Christ. But it is possible that the hesitation it conceals ('Art thou, really and fully, "he that should come" or are we to look even for "this same Jesus" again?') represents the single most potent factor in giving rise to the notion that the Christ was to come, not only once, but twice. Doubtless there were other, 'non-theological' factors— and apocalyptic is always in its way a response to non-theological factors. But while these colour the details (like 'the desolating sacrilege set up where it ought not to be' in Mark 13.14, or 'the man of lawlessness' and 'the restraining power' of II Thess. 2.3–12), it is difficult to see them as sufficient in themselves to have created the unprecedented notion of two comings of the Messiah. In the realm of the inner movement of ideas, I am inclined to think that what survives now as the extinct crater of Acts 3 provided once the volcanic power which, failing to find outlet in a heterodox Christology, erupted and coruscated in the surging spate of New Testament apocalyptic. But whether or not there is here any direct historical link, it may have its value as a dramatic representation. For one can, I believe, without distortion read the rest of the theology of the New Testament as an unresolved tension between the positions first adumbrated in the sermons of Acts 3 and Acts 2.

Another difference never wholly settled within the thinking of the early Church may also be traced to this same source.

The theology of the sermon in Acts 3 (though not of its setting) is a theology of the absentee Christ, inoperative in heaven; that in Acts 2 of the Christ presently active in his Church through the power of the Spirit. For Acts 3, the Christ is inoperative because he has not yet been sent, and there is no mention of the Spirit because its outpouring must wait upon the dawning of the messianic age, the coming of 'the times of refreshment'. In its doctrine of the Spirit, as in its doctrine of Christ, the actual position of Acts 3 was decisively rejected by the Church. But its influence may perhaps still be seen behind the abiding tension within Christian thinking between the 'while I was still with you' of Luke 24.44 and the 'lo, I am with you always' of Matt. 28.20. Luke, and the Church ever since, has held together the theology of a return after absence with one of an abiding presence; but the two conceptions go back, I believe, in origin to the divergent presuppositions of Acts 3 and Acts 2. That there could be any doubt whether the age of the Spirit had begun, suggests, as we should suspect, that the emphasis upon a separate and unmistakable event for the coming of the Spirit is part of Luke's theological construction, comparable with his treatment of the Ascension. Neither is so represented elsewhere in the New Testament. Originally, it would appear, the gift of the Spirit, like the exaltation of Christ, was associated with the Resurrection (as indeed Acts 2.33 itself suggests). Just as it was possible to doubt whether this event was itself the inauguration of the messianic reign, so it could seriously be questioned whether the age of the Spirit had yet dawned; for the final baptism of the Spirit belonged specifically to the One who was to come (Mark 1.7 f.; cf. Acts 19.1–4).

But we must return to the implications of the divergence between Acts 3 and Acts 2 for the coming of Christ.

The former position stems directly out of the Jewish messianic hope: in fact it *is* the Jewish messianic hope, with the modification that the Christ, when he comes, will be Jesus. One could, if one wished to, say that Acts 3 does speak of a *Parousia,* but of a Jewish *Parousia.* But this language would be misleading, for, as we have said, Judaism never used the word in connexion with the Messiah. Stephen's speech, working within the same frame of reference, correctly employs the term *eleusis,* not *parousia,* of the coming of the Righteous One (Acts 7.52). Moreover, while in Acts 3 the Messiah is reserved in heaven till the time of his appearing (as one line of Jewish expectation believed), there is no suggestion that, when he comes, he will descend from heaven on clouds of glory. In fact he will be 'sent' (Acts 3.20) exactly as the Servant has been 'sent' (3.26), and it would be merely confusing to speak of a *parousia* of either: each simply appears on earth in his due time. For a similar combination of heavenly pre-existence and earthly generation, we may compare the words of IV Ezra 12.32: 'This is the Messiah whom the Most High hath kept unto the end of the days, who shall spring from the seed of David, and shall come and speak unto them' that are on earth.[1]

This Jewish expectation, modified by the proclamation that Jesus is also the forerunner of the Christ he is to be, is internally quite consistent. The messianic event still lies wholly in the future. The disturbance of this frame of reference begins when, with Acts 2, the Apostles proclaim that the messianic age *has begun* with the Resurrection. What happens then to the traditional eschatology? One thing is clear: the final 'day of the Lord' has not yet arrived—for history goes on. Yet 'the last days' have begun, for with the outpouring of the Spirit the signs predicted by Joel as occurring 'before the day of the Lord comes' have been given. The powers of the age to come are already at work. The situation no longer requires repentance so that the Messiah may come (a typically Jewish conception), but repentance because the Messiah has come. There is still a waiting, a 'not yet'; but it is a waiting till all is reduced to the reign of the Christ. No more than in Acts 3 is there a second messianic event: such an idea had not yet been entertained.

[1]For other evidence in the same direction, *vide* Glasson, op. cit., pp. 222–5.

Yet the doubt persists: 'Has Jesus fully come as the Christ?' The sort of prophecies that filled the mind at any rate of the early Paul, that the Messiah would slay the wicked with the breath of his lips (Isa. 11.4; cited in II Thess. 2.8), had clearly *not* been fulfilled; and the more that the predictions about 'the Lord' of the Old Testament were applied to Jesus—such that he would 'come', 'and all his holy ones with him', in 'vengeance' and 'glory' (cf. I Thess. 3.13; II Thess. 1.7–10), the more pressing the need for a second messianic moment in which expectations not satisfied by his first coming could yet be met. And so the hope of a Christ to come (belonging originally to a purely Jewish, and then to a sub-Christian, theology of the messianic act) is retained alongside the hope of the eventual lordship of a Christ who has come. Instead of *all* being inaugurated, though only inaugurated, in the visitation and vindication of Jesus, some aspects of the promised messianic event are attached to the first coming, others (like judgement and the gathering of the elect) are deferred for a second. The differences of emphasis in New Testament theology represent the varying manner in which the significance of the Christ-event is distributed between these two moments.

For Paul the distinction between a first coming in great humility and a second in glorious majesty is relatively simple; for he has no theology of the Ministry in terms of glory. As Professor R. Bultmann has pointed out,[1] the words of John 12.28, 'I have glorified it (i.e., my name in Jesus), and I will glorify it again', would be unthinkable for Paul. For him there is no glorifying of Jesus again, but simply exaltation after emptying and poverty (Phil. 2.5–11).

The stronger, however, becomes the emphasis, such as we find progressively in the Gospels, that Jesus is the Christ, not merely by virtue of the Resurrection and in pre-existent glory, but in the lowliness of the Ministry itself, the more complicated the situation becomes. The problem of how to relate the glory of the 'first' coming to that of the 'second' can be seen rearing

[1] *The Theology of the New Testament*, II, p. 12.

its head in the later parts of the New Testament. With in-
creasing stress on the significance of the Incarnation, the same
words begin to seem appropriate to both comings. Once in
Paul—in a late epistle (Col. 1.26 and 3.4)—and once in I Peter
(1.20 and 5.4) the same verb 'to be manifested', is used of both.
And in the later books this double usage is more general. In the
Johannine writings 'to be manifested', like 'to come', is used
indifferently of the Incarnation and of the *Parousia*,[1] and in
the Pastoral Epistles 'the appearing' of Jesus Christ refers both
backwards and forwards.[2] In II Peter 1.16 'the power and
parousia of our Lord Jesus Christ' is seen as anticipated
already in the majesty of the Transfiguration; and in Ignatius
(*Philad.* ix, 2) 'the *parousia* of the Saviour, our Lord Jesus
Christ' can actually stand as a general description of the
ministry of Jesus.[3] From that it is a short step to the doctrine
of two *parousias,* with the use of the terms 'the first coming'
and 'the second coming', found for the first time in Justin
Martyr.[4]

[1] φανεροῦμαι: of the past in John 1.31; 21.1, 14; I John 1.2;
3.5,8; of the future in I John 2.28; 3.2; cf. John 14.21 f. (ἐμφανίζω).
    ἔρχομαι: of the past in John 1.11; 12.46 f.; 15.22; 16.28;
18.37, etc.; I John 4.2; 5.6; II John 7; of the future in John 14.3,
18, 23, 28; 21.22 f.; cf. I John 2.18 and 4.3 (of the Antichrist).
I John 5.6 probably contains a double reference—to the Incarnation
and to the coming of Christ in the sacraments (cf. below, p. 185).

[2] ἐπιφάνεια, ἐπιφαίνω: of the past in II Tim. 1.10; Tit. 2.11;
3.4; of the future in I Tim. 6.14; II Tim. 4.1, 8; Tit. 2.13.
φανεροῦμαι, interestingly, is in these Epistles used only of the
Incarnation: I Tim. 3.16; II Tim. 1.10; Tit. 1.3.

[3] How little it was a technical term still in the second century is
shown by the close juxtaposition in *Ep. Diognet.*, vii, 6 and 9 of
the words 'who shall endure his presence?' (viz., the future advent
of Christ) and 'the proofs of his presence' (viz., God's self-dis-
closure in the world).

[4] His phrases are: 'the two *parousias*' (*Apol.* lii, 3; *Dial.* xxxii, 2;
xl, 4; xlix, 2; lii, 1 and 4, etc.); 'the first and second *parousia*' (*Apol.*
lii, 3; *Dial.* xiv, 8; xl, 4; liv, 1; lxix, 7; cx, 2; etc.); 'his coming again'
(ἡ πάλιν παρουσία) (*Dial.* cxviii, 2). Justin also uses 'his *parousia*' by
itself for the 'first coming' of Jesus (*Apol.* xlviii, 2; liv, 7; *Dial.*
lxxxviii, 2; cxx, 3). Cf. Tertullian, *Adv. Marcion* iii, 7; *Apol.* xxi;

Prior to this formulation, the two lie together without co-ordination. Of this the Epistle to the Hebrews provides a good example. It is the Epistle in which the idea of a second coming is least integrated into the work as a whole, though, characteristically, it is also the one in which it comes to most explicit expression in the New Testament. The assertion that 'Christ . . . will appear a second time' is the nearest approach in any canonical writer to the later term 'the second coming'. But, fundamentally, the theology of the Epistle to the Hebrews is the fully inaugurated eschatology of Acts 2.

'As it is, we do not yet see everything in subjection to him [i.e. to man]. But we see Jesus, who for a little while was made lower than the angels, crowned with glory and honour because of the suffering of death' (2.8 f.).

'When Christ had offered for all time a single sacrifice for sins, he sat down at the right hand of God, thereafter[1] to wait until his enemies should be made a stool for his feet' (10.12 f.).

This is the only New Testament book specifically to use the language of inauguration, of the 'opening' of the new and living way (10.20), and the entire metaphysic of the writer presupposes a single final act charged with abiding and eternal consequences:

'He has been manifested once for all at the end of the age . . . now to appear in the presence of God' (9.24–6).

Such is the logic of the Epistle; and the subsequent phrase, 'And . . . he will be seen a second time' (9.27 f.)[2],

---

also *Clem, Recog.* I, 49 and 69; and the *Muratorian Canon* ll. 23–6: 'His twofold advent, the first in despised lowliness, which has taken place, and the second with kingly power, which is yet to come'.

[1]τὸ λοιπόν.

[2]The terms used are: πεφανέρωται; νῦν ἐμφανισθῆναι; ὀφθήσεται. It is interesting how the word here reserved for the *Parousia* is that originally applied to the Resurrection appearances (I Cor. 15.5–8). Cf. the use of the same word in Mark 13.26; 14.62; and 16.7 (also 9.4). There is a parallel use of φανεροῦμαι in the fourth Gospel of the appearances (John 21.1, 14) and in I John (2.28; 3.2) of the *Parousia*.

is not really integrated with the rest. This is not to say that it is incompatible; but it is related to the whole almost as loosely as the *Parousia* expectation of the Johannine postscript, 'What if he remain till I come?' (John 21.22), is related to the rest of the fourth Gospel. It belongs, I believe, properly to the other stream of thought (going back not to Acts 2 but to Acts 3), which required it precisely because it could not accept the fully inaugurated eschatology represented in the body alike of the Epistle to the Hebrews and the Gospel of John.

This brings us to the place of the fourth Gospel. From one point of view, it represents the conclusion of one of the two lines of development sketched in this chapter. For John, the glory of Christ has already dwelt among us so completely that no need or room is left for any second coming. The Christ who for Paul was shortly to come down from heaven (I Thess. 4.16) is for John the Christ who has come down from heaven (John 3.13; 6.38–58). Yet so to represent the fourth Gospel is to misrepresent it. It is doubtful, indeed, whether it can justly be treated simply as the last term of any development. For it stands in many ways as near to the source of the tradition as to its end. Like Paul, John bestrides the whole process of early Christian theology like a colossus—its *alpha* as much as its *omega*. We shall therefore devote a separate, and final, chapter to the Gospel of John, to see whether through it, and through the mature thought of Paul, we may come to a deeper understanding of the teaching of the New Testament as a whole.

But in closing we may sum up the theme of this chapter by way of an introduction to the last.

What we have been studying is the splitting of a unity rather than the deliberate creation of a duality. That is to say, the doctrine of the Second Coming does not represent the tacking on of another clause to the Christian Creed, the addition of a futurist element to a gospel that originally knew no such hope. In that case, it would be a very questionable element in Christian Faith, and we should prepare to shed it as an extraneous accretion. On the contrary, all that lies at the heart of the *Parousia* doctrine was already there in the teaching of Jesus and the preaching of the primitive Church. The only question was how this element—the element of the here-after—was properly to be expressed. And the very ambiguity of the word 'hereafter' conceals the hesitation which the Church has felt ever since. 'Hereafter you will see the Son of man seated at the right hand of Power and coming on the clouds of heaven': so runs the familiar version of 1611, trans-lating a phrase which signifies unequivocally 'from now on'—literally '*here*after'. But it is safe to say that it is generally understood to mean something very different—not 'hence-forth', but 'in the hereafter', 'at some point in the indefinite future'. The content of the expectation there expressed re-mains the same—the final sovereignty of the Christ in glory. The question concerns merely the moment at which this is conceived as inaugurated. The element represented by the *Parousia* idea is not alien. The only issue is whether we are prepared to take Jesus and the primitive gospel at their word and say that this, like all else contained in the Christ-event, is now no longer *simply* future but also present. The conception of a second coming distinct from the first is not the result of adding something to the gospel which did not belong to it. It arose because the gospel was too big, not because it was not big enough; because its wholeness could not be contained, and its unity came to be broken. It may even be that for our minds something of the sort is inevitable: the Christian hope must have a basis in the picture, at any rate, of a separate event, and require, for its definition, a second focus. But much distortion and not a little sheer fantasy and perversion has resulted from a one-sided Adventism. We owe it to the Church and to our-selves to try to recover the wholeness of the Christian hope, to find again the unity of the Christ who has come and of the Christ who shall come in the Christ who comes. It is that task to which we shall address ourselves in the closing chapter.

8

THE CHRIST WHO COMES

IT was suggested in the previous chapter that the story of
New Testament theology could, from one point of view, be
written round the crisis in Christology associated with the
question, 'Art thou "he that should come" or are we to look for
another?' There was never a doubt that it was to Jesus that the
Church should look, though the preservation twice in the
Markan material (Mark 13.5 f.; 21–3) as well as in 'Q' (Matt.
24.26; Luke 17.23) of warnings against false Christs suggests
that this was not a danger that could be ignored. But in what
sense he was 'the Coming One' was far from resolved. Had
Jesus fully come as the Christ?

One line of expectation, which finds men in the middle of
the second century still posing the question, 'Where is the
promise of his coming?' (II Peter 3.4), was that which led to
the composition of the New Testament apocalypses and is
most clearly represented in the Gospels by Matthew. It is that
of the earlier Paul,[1] and can perhaps be traced in origin to the
position of Acts 3, though the recognition of this strand is, of

[1]The whole question of the development of Paul's eschatology
is one of the continuing debates of New Testament theology. The
cases for and against development are set out in the articles by
C. H. Dodd from *The Bulletin of the John Rylands Library* reprinted
in his *New Testament Studies*, especially pp. 109–18, and J. Lowe in
The Journal of Theological Studies, XLII (1941), pp. 129–42. Cf.
W. L. Knox, *St Paul and the Church of the Gentiles,* chapter VI. I
believe that there *is* a real transition to be seen, though not with
any such radical break as both Dodd and Knox detect between I and
II Corinthians. But this is misconceived if understood, as it often is,

course, quite independent of the construction I ventured to put upon that speech. To this way of thinking, the Christ-event was still as much future as past: the messianic act was now, as it were, half way through.

Another strain of thought, fastening less on expectations left over from the Old Testament, and grounding itself on the decisive character of the Gospel events, expressed its hope rather in what we have called an *inaugurated* eschatology. It looked, that is to say, not for another coming of Christ, but to the certain reduction of all things to the Christ who had come, and whose 'coming to his own', alike in victory and in visitation, was *from now on* the ultimate and most pressing reality with which men must reckon. This is the strain represented, we argued, by Acts 2 and the primitive preaching generally, as well as by the earlier state of the Synoptic tradition. It is reflected in the Epistle to the Hebrews, and given classic expression in the fourth Gospel.

It would be entirely false to represent these alternatives as completely divergent or mutually incompatible. This is shown by the fact that they lie side by side, as we saw, in the Epistle to the Hebrews and the fourth Gospel, and even more obviously in the Johannine Epistles. Again, within the Pauline writings there is clear but gradual transition from one to the other. Indeed, at the two extremes, II Thessalonians and Ephesians (neither of which I yet see sufficient reason to deny to be Pauline) could well be cited as typically representative of the contrast between one way of thinking and the other.

---

as the abandonment of an eschatological way of thinking for a non-eschatological or 'mystical' outlook. The change is to be described rather as a shift from an apocalyptic to a non-apocalyptic form of eschatology. This is the reverse development to that which previously we detected in the Synoptic Gospels. What is early in Paul is late in the Synoptists, and by the time this way of thinking had come to affect the Synoptic tradition it had been left behind by Paul. The later Paul is, I believe, more faithful to the original tradition, and it is at this point also, as we shall see, that he comes closest to the thought of the fourth Gospel.

J.C.—L

Furthermore, Matthew, whose every tendency is to heighten
the element of apocalyptic and in whose Gospel the developed
Parousia doctrine finds its most explicit expression, nevertheless closes, as we have seen, upon words of the exalted Christ
which express as succinctly as any the theme of an eschatology
fully inaugurated from the Resurrection onwards.

However, false as it would be to exaggerate the divergence,
there can be little doubt that the two lines of thought do end,
and I would think also begin, at very different points. The
position of II Peter is not the same as that of the fourth Gospel,
nor is the conclusion of Ephesians that of II Thessalonians.

But what of the Gospel of John? We have not employed
it hitherto as evidence either of the teaching of Jesus or of
the mind of the Church. But it would be wholly misleading to
think of it as representing a standpoint which requires it to be
viewed in isolation from all the other New Testament documents. Indeed, more than enough injustice has already been
done by the practice, rational enough no doubt to the Liberal
critics but now becoming a dangerous habit, of treating the
fourth Gospel in separation from the other three and indeed
from the common proclamation behind them all. This has
contributed to the view that the Gospel represents, particularly in the matter of eschatology, a position which, if not
unique in the New Testament, is at any rate very much on one
wing of its thinking. I am convinced, on the contrary, that it
does not set forth a view of the End with a balance, or lack of
it, all its own, but, rather, an inaugurated eschatology in all
essentials identical with that of the primitive preaching, and
indeed also with that of Jesus himself as we have sought to
reconstruct it from the earliest strands of the Synoptic tradition. Indeed, if it were not for the constant explanation that
would have been required, I should have preferred to use its
evidence alongside that of our other sources.

I can here simply state two convictions about the nature of
that evidence which it would take us too far afield to argue in
detail. The first is that this Gospel is grounded in the same
common stock of Church tradition, often in a very early form,

from which the Synoptic material is drawn, and, with proper caution, can be used in the total reconstruction of the eschatological teaching of Jesus. It does not represent an entirely isolated and eccentric tradition, but one that in origin has as much and as primitive connexion with Palestinian soil— especially southern Palestinian soil—as any of the other material.[1] But, secondly, it is not, I believe, dependent on the Synoptic Gospels.[2] St John's Gospel is usually represented as a thorough-going re-editing, or transmuting, of the more apocalyptic eschatology of the Synoptists.[3] My own investigations suggest rather that he is not issuing a corrective of other views so much as setting forth, as Dr Dodd has hinted,[4] a tradition of the teaching of Jesus which had never seriously undergone the tendency towards apocalyptic that we have seen reason to regard as a potent factor of distortion.

I cannot do more than state these convictions here, and trust that they may to some extent be borne out in the subsequent argument. But it might help to interpose, without making any attempt to substantiate, the kind of picture of the place of the Johannine literature presupposed by the treatment that follows. For it runs counter to the general assumption that the Johannine eschatology is the result of a deliberate 'refining away'[5] of a 'cruder' apocalyptic tradition. On the contrary, I would trace in the writings ascribed to St John precisely the opposite process, and see in them the gradual subjection of a

[1]This assessment was reached independently of, but is now substantially strengthened by, the evidence of the Dead Sea Scrolls. *Vide,* e.g., W. F. Albright, 'Recent Discoveries in Palestine and the Gospel of St John' in *The Background of the New Testament and its Eschatology* (ed. W. D. Davies and D. Daube), pp. 153–71.

[2]Cf. P. Gardner-Smith, *St John and the Synoptic Gospels.*

[3]This estimate of John as a 'supreme and final corrective . . . couched in the form of a gospel', and therefore as salutary but one-sided, underlies, and I believe distorts, the otherwise suggestive treatment of Fison's book, *The Christian Hope* (e.g., pp. 145, 162, 179).

[4]*The Interpretation of the Fourth Gospel,* p. 447.

[5]Cf. Dodd's earlier work, *The Apostolic Preaching and its Developments,* p. 155 (original edition).

primitive non-apocalyptic eschatology to a subsequent and more apocalyptic way of thinking.

If one had to construct a picture—which the evidence cannot be sufficient to prove—I should be inclined to say that the tradition behind the fourth Gospel, preserved in circles which had entered Christianity under the influence of the Baptist (cf. John 1.35–9), and indirectly, therefore, of the outlook of the Qumran Community,[1] never moved far from its cradle in Judaea until the time of the Jewish war. At that time, we may suppose, it found refuge in its traditional home at Ephesus, where later the Johannine Epistles were written and where it was exposed to the influences of apocalyptic, which were to dominate it in the book of the Revelation. There seems to me now very little to *rule out* the view that the Gospel was in substance composed relatively early,[2] and was only edited and published at a later date in Asia Minor. Chapter 21, with its reference to the *Parousia* expectation, may have been added partly under the impact of the other stream of thought, which is quite evident in the Epistles. If these are distinct in time and circumstance from the Gospel, this *may* be sufficient to explain the differences which have compelled some commentators[3] to deny the unity of authorship.

Meanwhile, the apocalyptic tradition, which there is some evidence in Judaism for associating with Galilee and the north, may possibly have established itself in Christianity at Antioch, and from there made its way westwards. It was this Church from which Paul worked as a missionary during his 'apocalyptic' period, and whose theology, if B. H. Streeter is right (*The Four Gospels*, pp. 500–23), was later incorporated in the Gospel of Matthew. This might explain the connexions which we observed between Paul and Matthew (pp. 108–11

---

[1] *Vide* my forthcoming article, 'The Baptism of John and the Qumran Community', *Harvard Theological Review*, 1957.

[2] Cf. E. R. Goodenough, 'John a Primitive Gospel', *Journal of Biblical Literature*, LXIV (1945), pp. 145–82.

[3] Notably Dodd, *The Johannine Epistles* (Moffatt Commentary), pp. xlvii–lvi.

above), and to which Dr Dodd has also drawn attention.[1] It is interesting to observe that the Pauline and Johannine traditions come closest to meeting in two documents (not, I believe, so very distant in date of composition) which subsequent tradition associates with Ephesus, the Epistle to the Ephesians and the Gospel of John. The last state of the Pauline tradition has affinities with the earliest of the Johannine, just as the earliest elements in Paul correspond to the latest, editorial elements in Matthew.

But it must be emphasized that any such reconstruction is highly speculative. In any case, where the fourth Evangelist derived his material is not here our primary interest, and there is no need to prejudge the issue. Our concern is rather with what he made of it. For, even more than in any historical reliability that may attach to his sources, the value of John's presentation lies in the fact that with unique penetration he brings into creative unity elements in the common tradition which elsewhere tend to fall apart and thus become distorted. John is not presenting a different eschatology from that of the rest of the New Testament: he is seeing it whole.

Now, there are three points at least at which the fourth Gospel holds together elements never fully integrated in other parts of the New Testament, and at which therefore it may be able to help us to a more coherent statement of the Christian hope for ourselves.

(1) In the first place, it comprehends within a single and massive theological whole all the different facets of the act of God in Christ. One of the notable features of the primitive preaching was precisely its refusal to break up this unity. For it there was no distinction between the Resurrection and Ascension; the giving of the Spirit was closely linked with the exaltation of Jesus to the Father; and, as we have seen, the Christian hope was grounded not in a separate, future event but in the lordship of Christ already inaugurated at the Resurrection.

[1]'Matthew and Paul', reprinted from the *Expository Times* in his *New Testament Studies,* pp. 53–66.

This same unity at a deeper and even more inclusive level is characteristic of the fourth Gospel. For here the Cross as well as the Resurrection is included within the exaltation or glorification of Christ. It is no longer a case of, 'You killed Jesus by hanging him on a tree: God exalted him at his right hand' (Acts 5.30 f.). The whole is a single act of 'lifting up', which receives its most succinct and ironic expression in John 8.28: 'When you have lifted up the Son of man, then you will know that I am he'. The exaltation of Jesus remains for John the act of the Father *par excellence*. Yet it is identical with, and not merely subsequent to, the act of the Jews: for it is they, through the agency of the Romans, who will lift him up from the earth. Moreover, this single 'hour' of exaltation to which the whole ministry of Jesus points embraces proleptically all the 'signs' which prefigure it and the 'glory' which it casts before. There is no exclusive contrast, as in the Pauline preaching, between the moment of exaltation and the previous humiliation.

This single redemptive act is marked by such overwhelming theological unity that any distinction between its different moments is entirely subordinate. To characterize it, John retains, in order to deepen, the language of the primitive message. In it God 'glorifies' his Son;[1] in it Jesus is 'exalted',[2] and ascends,[3] and in it the Spirit is given.[4] The Passion is the

---

[1] John 7.39; 8.54; 12.16, 23; 13.31 f.; 17.1, 5; cf. Acts 3.13; and the very primitive 'gave him glory' of I Peter 1.21.

[2] John 3.14; 8.28; 12.32, 34; cf. Acts 2.33; 5.31.

[3] John 3.13; 6.62; 20.17; cf. Acts 2.34. The use of ἀναβαίνω throughout the Gospel for 'going up' to Jerusalem is almost certainly charged with theological significance. This comes out most clearly in the sequence in 7.1–14: ' "Show yourself to the world" . . . Jesus said . . . "I am not going up to *this* feast, for my time has not yet fully come".' The hour of his ἀνάβασις is not yet. Cf. the similar double usage in Luke 9.51 ('When therefore the days drew near for him to be received up, he set his face to go to Jerusalem'); 18.31; 19.28.

[4] John 7.39; 19.30 (?); 20.22; cf. John 15.26 with Acts 2.33, where in both passages the promised Spirit is viewed as sent by Jesus from the Father as a direct result of his exaltation.

decisive, the eschatological moment, when the world is judged (12.31) and the end is reached (13.1) and all things are finished (19.28–30).

'The hour for the Son of man to be glorified', which comes when the 'grain of wheat falls into the earth and dies' (12. 23 f.), combines and fuses in its phraseology two moments which in the Synoptists get separated: it is not only the 'hour' of the Passion, of which Mark also speaks (cf. John 12.27 and Mark 14.35); it is 'the day when the Son of man is revealed' (Luke 17.30) and 'sits on his throne of glory' (Matt. 19.28; 25.31).[1] The Markan saying at the Trial, 'You will see the Son of man sitting at the right hand of power and coming with the clouds of heaven' (14.62) is echoed both in the question, 'What if you were to see the Son of man ascending where he was before?' (John 6.62),[2] and in the prediction, 'When you have lifted up the Son of man, then you will know that I am he' (8.28), which receives its anticipatory and ironical fulfilment in 19.5, when Pilate leads out Jesus in regal glory, and, in the sight of the chief priests, says to the Jews: 'Behold, the Man!' The reference of these sayings in John is clearly to the Passion, as the moment inaugurating the glory, and his interpretation of this as a going to God[3] reflects what we argued to be the

[1]John stresses the Passion as the moment when the King is crowned and invested with the royal purple (19.2–5), and 19.13 f. may be deliberately and ironically ambiguous: 'Pilate led out Jesus καὶ ἐκάθισεν ἐπὶ βήματος ("sat down on the judgement seat" or "set him on the judgement seat") . . . and said to the Jews, Behold your king!' C. K. Barrett comments: 'We may suppose that John meant that Pilate did in fact sit on the βῆμα, but that for those with eyes to see behind this human scene appeared the Son of man, to whom all judgement has been committed (5.22), seated upon his throne' (*St John*, ad loc.).

[2]The *context* of this saying, spoken to the disciples and preceded by the words, 'Do you take offence at this?' makes it parallel rather with the situation in Mark 8.31–9.1. We have already seen reason to believe that for Jesus, as originally for Mark, the rising of the Son of man out of suffering and death and the coming of the Son of man with the clouds are alternative expressions for the same thing. They are certainly so interpreted by John.

[3]7.33; 13.3; 14.12, 28; 16.5, 10, 17, 28; 17.11, 13.

original meaning of the Markan saying, that it spoke of a coming to God in ascent and vindication.[1]

In all this there is an unequivocal assertion that the climax of the Ministry itself in the exaltation of Jesus out of death is the decisive event upon which everything turns. This is the emphasis which we detected in Jesus' own teaching, but which is obscured in the Synoptic Gospels by the introduction of a second focus. There the moments of sitting at the right hand of God and of coming on the clouds of heaven begin to fall apart: in John they are inseparably one.

(2) To insist upon this unity alone would, however, be to give an entirely one-sided picture of the theology of the Gospel. This is indeed what is frequently done. It is represented as setting forth a completely 'realized' eschatology, in which nothing remains of future expectation except a few dim shadows of a final day and an occasional concession to the traditional viewpoint. Thus portrayed, the Johannine picture would certainly be unrepresentative of the New Testament, and to use it in any way as a summary of the whole would be seriously to distort the perspective. Indeed, it is probable that

---

[1] I am much attracted by the suggestion put to me by Professor W. Manson that John 1.51, 'Truly, truly, I say to you, you will see heaven opened, and the angels of God ascending and descending to [ἐπί + acc.] the Son of man', is another such prediction of vindication. If the allusion is to Gen. 28.12, the Son of man is then conceived not *as* the ladder, nor at the bottom of it (during the Incarnation), but at the top. Like 6.62, it is to be read as a prediction of the greater things to be seen when the Son of man ascends where he was before. Its language, however, would echo the *other* half of the Trial saying, and expand the idea of subjection *to* the Son of man implied in the quotation from Ps. 110.1. It might then provide a foundation in the words of Jesus for the theme which recurs in the primitive credal summaries, of the angelic powers both from the heights and from the depths paying their homage to the exalted Christ (Phil. 2.10; I Pet. 3.18–22; Eph. 1.20 f.; I Tim. 3.16). Alternatively, if the emphasis is not on subjection but on the traffic between heaven and earth, it would refer to the living way to be opened henceforth by the exaltation of the Son of man, as in Heb. 10.12–20.

I shall not be able in a single chapter to dispel the prejudgement that this is precisely what I am doing.

Now one of the features, again, of the primitive preaching was its preservation of an essential unity between the 'now' and 'not yet'. In its formula 'from now on' it declined to set any gulf between the inauguration of the messianic reign and its consummation in the ultimate reduction of all things to Christ. There were not two events, but a single once and for all event inaugurating a process.

This unity is also a marked characteristic of the fourth Gospel. Indeed, it is precisely because it is preserved so closely that the impression can be given that the element of 'not yet' is unrepresented. It is, to be sure, not represented as a separate and distinct moment, in the kind of *Parousia* which isolates and gathers into a second dramatic event every element which yet awaits fulfilment. But such a moment appears only when the theology of a fully inaugurated eschatology has already been broken into one in which some things are wholly finished and others wholly future.

Let us then examine the way in which the Gospel of John retains and expresses this second unity, between the 'now' and 'not yet'.

In the first place, the Johannine Christ, like the Jesus of the Synoptists, speaks unambiguously of a 'last day', which will be marked by the general Resurrection (6.39 f., 44, 54; 11.24; cf. 5.28 f.) and final Judgement (12.48; cf. 5.28 f.). This is not simply a residual element in the theology of the Gospel. It is, to be sure, little mentioned, but for precisely the same reason, and to much the same degree, as it is little mentioned in the Synoptists. It represents a horizon to the teaching of Jesus which is already so familiar to his audience, and is so unchallenged, that it can naturally remain in the background. What occupies the foreground in both is the great new factor introduced into the existing framework by the life, death and resurrection of Jesus himself.

Yet that new factor is strictly only *introduced* with the coming of Jesus: it is something that *has come* into the world, from then on—not merely as a once and for all event, now over, but as an abiding event. Thus it comes about that the perfect is the characteristic tense of the Gospel; and that perfect implies both a present and a future: 'the hour is coming and now is' (4.23; 5.25; cf. 16.32). This is the rubric by which the whole theology of John must be interpreted, and by which he holds together, as no other Evangelist does, the period of the Incarnation and the period of the Church. There is an important sense, indeed, in which this formula applies in the first instance to the period of the ministry of Jesus itself, when, to use the language of the Synoptists, the Kingdom is already exercising its 'powers' but has still to 'come with power'. But this continues to be the truth in a different sense of the whole period between the Resurrection and the Last Day. Here too all is inaugurated, yet only inaugurated: there is an already, but there is also a not yet. 'He who eats my flesh and drinks my blood has eternal life'; but this must immediately be followed by the word: 'And I will raise him up at the last day.'[1]

Nowhere is this balance more carefully preserved than in John's treatment of the Judgement, which is representative of his whole eschatology. The last Judgement has even now been introduced into the world by 'the coming of the Son of man' in the ministry of Jesus (9.39; 5.27). As in the primitive preaching, Jesus has already been designated judge by God (5.27). For the early preaching, this designation, like all the others, took place at the Resurrection (Acts 10.42; 17.31). But just as in Mark Jesus claims, as Son of man, already on earth to be exercising his authority as judge in the forgiveness of sins (2.10), so, for John, the very presence of the Son of man among men is a passing of judgement. Like all else, this reaches its climax in his death, which is *par excellence* the judgement of this world, in the double and typically Johannine sense, of the judgement passed by the world and the judgement passed upon the world (12.31; 16.11). In a true sense, then, the last Judgement has already occurred:

[1] 6.54; cf. 11.23–7, and the characteristic combination of fulfilment and promise in 12.28, 31; 13.31 f.; 14.17; 17.26.

'He who believes in him is not condemned; he who does not believe is condemned already, because he has not believed in the name of the only Son of God. And this is the judgement, that the light has come into the world, and men loved darkness rather than light' (3.18 f.).

Yet the judgement, here begun, has still a future reference:

'He who rejects me and does not receive my sayings has a judge; the word that I have spoken will be his judge on the last day' (12.48; cf. Mark 8.38; Luke 12.9 = Matt. 10.33),

and 'the hour' is yet 'coming'

'when all who are in the tombs will hear the voice of the Son of man and will come forth, those who have done good, to the resurrection of life, and those who have done evil, to the resurrection of judgement' (5.28 f.).

This last is pure apocalyptic, with a clear echo of Dan. 12.2. And it introduces the question of what John does with that element which looms so large both in the Synoptic and Pauline eschatology.

The function of apocalyptic is precisely to make the link we are discussing between the present and the future, to relate the things that are to 'the things that must be hereafter' (Rev. 4.1). Yet, as we saw earlier, its very method led historically to the breaking-up of that integration of final significance and present event which was so characteristic of the outlook of the Prophets. Eschatology ceased to be an interpretation of present history: it became a study of supra-historical occurrences in the future. In the same way, when applied to the teaching of Jesus, the processes of apocalyptic thinking dissipated the unity of the earliest preaching. The single eschatological act of God introduced into history 'from now on' became split into a series of historical events, to be followed after an interval by a purely supernatural climax, separated from them in time and discontinuous in conception. The Synoptic apocalypses, which are concerned with what must take place after the death of Jesus, in fact effectively break the original unity of these things with what did take place *in* the death of

Jesus. Events like the destruction of Jerusalem and the persecution of the disciples, which for Jesus were part of the meaning of his visitation and the direct outcome of his rejection, become interpreted by, and indeed parts of, another complex of events lying still in the future. What must happen because the Son of man has come is turned into what must happen before the Son of man can come.

This is the process which we detected at work upon the Synoptic material. From this process the fourth Gospel is entirely free. Yet it is just as much concerned with what must happen hereafter. It too speaks, in 16.13, of 'the things that are to come'; and the occurrence of this phrase in the Last Discourses should serve as a reminder that these discourses perform precisely the same function as the Synoptic apocalypses. They also are an answer to the question: 'Tell us, when will this be, and what will be the sign when these things are all to be accomplished?' (Mark 13.4). The sign will be the last and greatest 'sign', of the Son of man lifted up from the earth; and in this all will be 'accomplished' (John 19.28). Practically all the themes of the Synoptic discourse are here represented—the injunction against alarm, the forewarning against apostasy, the prediction of travail and tribulation and of persecution for the sake of the name, the need for witness, the promise of the Spirit as the disciples' advocate, the reference to 'that day', when, in an imminent coming, Christ will be seen and manifested, the elect will be gathered to him, and the world will be judged.[1]

---

[1]*Alarm*: John 14.1, 27; cf. Mark 13.7, 11; *apostasy*: John 13.18 f.; 16.1, 4; cf. Mark 13.5 f.; 21–3; Rev. 2.2; *travail*: John 16.20–2; cf. Mark 13.8; *tribulation*: John 16.33; cf. Mark 13.19; Rev. 2.9 f.; *persecution for the sake of the name*: John 15.18–21; 16.2; cf. Mark 13.9, 12 f.; Luke 21.12, 16 f.; Matt. 10.17 f., 21–5; Rev. 2.3; *the need for witness*: John 15.27; cf. Mark 13.9; Luke 21.13; *the Spirit as advocate*: John 14.26; 15.26; 16.13; cf. Mark 13.11; Matt. 10.20; Luke 12.12; *that day*: John 14.20; 16.23, 26; cf. Mark 13.32 and 13.17, 19, 24; *imminent*: John 14.19; 16.16–19; cf. Mark 13.20; Rev. 2.16; 3.11; *coming*: John 14.3, 18, 23, 28; cf. Mark 13.26; Rev. 1.7; *seen*: John 14.19; 16.16–19, 22; cf. Mark 13.26; Rev. 1.7;

These are the classic themes of the apocalypses. Yet here they all are in John, linked not with a second supernatural event but with the single historical crisis of the death and resurrection of Jesus. This is the *telos,* the End; and its tense is no longer the future (Matt. 24.14; Mark 13.7) but the perfect (John 19.28, 30).[1] *This,* and not something yet to appear in the skies, is the final 'sign' of the Son of man, when, to supply the Old Testament background, as 'an ensign for the nations' to 'assemble the outcasts of Israel',[2] Jesus is 'lifted up' like the serpent in the wilderness, to 'gather into one the children of God who are scattered abroad'.[3] Again, it is *in* the death of Christ itself and not merely after it, that, for John, the Temple is destroyed (John 2.18–21; cf. Mark 13.1–4). All these things are not exhausted in this event, but they are initiated by it: there is no other focus in the Gospel to which they can be attached.[4]

This unity between the fulfilled and the future is most succinctly illustrated in the last occurrence of the formula, 'the

---

manifested: John 14.21; cf. Matt. 24.27, 30; Luke 17.24, 30; *elect*: John 15.16; cf. Mark 13.20, 27; *gathered to him*: John 14.3; 11.52; cf. Mark 13.27; *the world will be judged*: John 16.8–11; cf. Matt. 24.30; 25.31–46.

[1] Contrast also the meaning of 'to the end' in Mark 13.13; Rev. 2.26 and in John 13.1.

[2] Isa. 11.12. For the 'sign' of the Son of man in Matt. 24.30 f. as the 'ensign' of Old Testament prophecy, *vide* Glasson, op. cit., pp. 189–91; and Beasley-Murray, op. cit., pp. 259 f. (cf. especially its combination with the trumpet in Isa. 18.3: 'When a signal is raised on the mountains, look! When a trumpet is blown, hear!').

[3] John 3.14; 11.52. In Num. 21.8 f. Moses sets up the brazen serpent on a standard, ἐπὶ σημείου.

[4] This is the decisive difference. In *The Gospel Message of St Mark,* chapter IV, R. H. Lightfoot made a gallant effort to demonstrate an integral connexion between Mark's eschatological discourse and the ensuing Passion narrative. But, apart from the fact that the parallels are often forced, Mark 13, as it stands at the moment, is dominated by a second focus, which must draw the attention of the reader, unless he be of quite perverse ingenuity, *away* from the Passion to the *Parousia.*

hour is coming and now is', though here, in the Last Discourses, where, as Dr Dodd has emphasized,[1] Jesus speaks,
as it were, from the other side of the Passion, the 'now' of
present process has given place to the perfect of completed
action:

'The hour is coming, indeed it has come, when you will be scattered,
every man to his home, and will leave me alone' (16.32).

This saying once more brings together two moments which in
the Synoptists are separate, as indeed in temporal sequence
they were: the moment when at the Passion the disciples are
dispersed and flee (Mark 14.27,50) and the days when after the
Passion they must again be dispersed and flee (Luke 21.12–24).
Whereas the other Gospels link this latter moment, by way of
prelude, to an event yet to take place, in John it is part of the
same event in which the Son of man is himself delivered up:[2]
the time for it both is coming and has come. In the same way,
'the *beginning* of the pangs', or messianic woes, lies not, as in
the Synoptists, *after* the death of Jesus (Mark 13.8), but *in* the
death of Jesus (John 16.20–2). It is here that the travail is set
in motion: all that follows is but the outworking of that.

[1] *The Interpretation of the Fourth Gospel*, pp. 397 f. My indebtedness to this masterly treatment of the theology of the Gospel will be
apparent throughout.

[2] T. W. Manson, in his essay, 'Realized Eschatology and the
Messianic Secret', *Studies in the Gospels* (ed. D. E. Nineham), pp.
218 f., draws attention to the repeated parallels in Jesus' language
between what must befall the Son of man and what must befall the
disciples: 'The Son of man is delivered up (Mark 9.31): so are the
disciples (13.9, 11). He is brought before the authorities (8.31;
10.33): so are they (Mark 13.9; cf. Luke 12.11). He is treated with
hatred and contempt (8.31; 9.12): the disciples may expect the
same treatment (Mark 13.13; Luke 10.16; cf. Matt. 5.11, Luke 6.22).
He is scourged (Mark 10.34); so are the disciples (13.9; cf. Matt. 10.
17). He is put to death (8.31; 9.31; 10.34): the disciples are re-
peatedly warned that they must be prepared for the same fate
(8.34 f.; cf. Matt. 10.38 f.; Luke 14.27; 17.33).' This association
between his own passion and that of his disciples is almost certainly
an original mark of Jesus' teaching, and it is John who best preserves
it.

It is this indissoluble unity between the 'now' and the 'not yet' which enables the fourth Evangelist to treat the *Parousia* itself in the same way. Nowhere more seriously than at this point was the original unity disrupted. What was for Jesus at his Trial a coming affirmed from the moment of the Passion onwards became dissociated from the Paschal events altogether. The *Parousia* came to be placed the other side of an ever-widening chasm posted at intervals with such warnings as: 'Not yet' (Mark 13.7); 'Not immediately' (Luke 21.9; cf. 19.11); 'Remember, with the Lord one day is as a thousand years' (II Peter 3.8).

Once again, John does not excise the element represented in the *Parousia* hope. It is all there: in fact there are more sayings of Jesus about a future coming in John than there are in Mark.

'I will come again and will take you to myself' (14.3).

'I will come to you. Yet a little while and the world will see me no more, but you will see me' (14.18 f.).

'I go away, and I will come to you' (14.28).

'A little while, and you will see me no more; again a little while, and you will see me' (16.16).

'You have sorrow now, but I will see you again' (16.22).[1]

There is no more explicit language in the New Testament. In fact only here does the idea of coming *again*, which, like the phrase 'the second coming', plays such a large part in our modern speech, receive any emphasis at all: elsewhere it is always simply 'the coming' of Christ, not his return.

Indeed, it is possibly here, if anywhere, that we should seek the foundation in the words of Jesus for the promise of his coming.[2] The words, 'A little while and you will see me',

---

[1] The saying in the postscript, 'What if he remain till I come' (21.22), cannot be regarded as integral to the theology of the Gospel. It is in any case introduced as an example of traditional expectation which needs to be rescued from misunderstanding. I suggested earlier (p. 91) that it was to be associated with the kind of development which may have overtaken Mark 9.1.

[2] This suggestion was made to me by the Reverend H. W. Montefiore.

'because I go to the Father' (16.17), are remarkably like the assurance given by Jesus to the disciples in Mark that 'after he is raised' they will 'see' him 'as he said' (Mark 14.28; 16.7). Together with the coming on the clouds predicted at the Trial and the visitation of the Son of man in the hour of the nation's crisis, this could be enough to provide the dominical basis for the subsequent development. But upon the lips of Jesus this language describes no second eschatological moment after an interval, but the consummation and fruition of that which is now being brought to fulfilment. In Mark, we have urged, this unitary conception of the *Parousia* was originally preserved, but subsequently disrupted. In John it is never broken: no division is introduced between the different elements.

Just as the coming of Christ to the Father coincides with the coming of the Spirit (John 7.39),[1] so the coming of Jesus to the disciples is indistinguishable from the coming of the Paraclete (15.26; 16.7 f., 13; 20.19–22), and in one passage is even associated with the coming of the Father (14.23). The *Parousia* is clearly understood not as a separate catastrophic occurrence, but as a continuous pervasion of the daily life of the disciple and the Church. The coming is an abiding presence, 'We will come to him and make our home with him' (14.23), exactly as in the parting promise of Matthew's Gospel: 'Lo, I am with you always, to the close of the age' (28.20). It is the Passion which makes possible and inaugurates the *Parousia from now on*. The going of Christ to the Father itself initiates the coming of Christ from the Father.[2]

[1] Also 19.30, if, with Hoskyns and Davey (*The Fourth Gospel*, ad loc.) we may see in παρέδωκεν τὸ πνεῦμα both 'he gave up his spirit' and 'he handed over the Spirit'.

[2] O. Cullmann, in 'The Return of Christ', *The Early Church*, p. 154 f. n. 13, speaks of 'the three modes of the Lord's return' in the Gospel of John—'his coming as the risen one, his coming in the Paraclete, and his coming at the end of time'—and adds: 'This third eschatological coming in the fourth Gospel must not be suppressed; such a mutilation would entail the arbitrary suppression of a great number of verses'. But, with all due respect, there is not a single text in the Gospel which associates 'the last day' with the *coming*

(3) This introduces the third point at which the fourth Evangelist preserves and deepens a unity constantly imperilled in the rest of the tradition.

We distinguished earlier two ideas involved in the meaning of the *Parousia,* those of vindication and of visitation, of ascent to God and descent from God. Both of these, we insisted, were integral to the conception and neither must be sacrificed or separated. Yet, in fact, elsewhere in the New Testament they are seriously separated, the thought of vindication becoming attached to one moment—the Resurrection and the Ascension—and that of visitation to another.

Luke, as we have seen, seeks to harmonize and rationalize the divergent traditions by speaking of two similar events, one after the other:

'This Jesus, who was taken up from you into heaven, will come in the same way as you saw him go' (Acts 1.11).

But in John it is not merely that the manner of two separate events will be the same; they are the same event—the Resurrection inaugurating the *Parousia*—looked at from two points of view, of coming to the Father in vindication and coming from the Father in power. This unity was originally present, as we saw, in the primitive preaching in Acts 2.33: 'Being therefore exalted at the right hand of God, and having received from the Father the promise of the Holy Spirit, he has poured out this which you see and hear'. But subsequently it became quite overlaid.[1] The immediacy of the vindication was retained, the imminence of the visitation was gradually protracted. But John insists that the 'three days' which mark the period of restoration (2.19–22) are the same 'little while' within

---

of Christ. It would be possible to take 14.3 to refer to 'the end of time', but in the context of the other sayings, this appears improbable.

[1]The connexion between the ascension of Christ to the Father and his gifts to men reappears in Eph. 4.8–10, an Epistle which in its eschatology has striking affinities with the fourth Gospel; cf. John 3.13, 31, 34.

which Jesus is to be restored to the disciples (16.16–22). And it is not simply that the length of the interval is the same: he will see them again *because* he is going to the Father. The one movement is completed only in the other. Jesus comes to his own in visitation, only as he comes to his own in glory; the Ascension is finished only when contact with the disciples is re-established.[1] For the Ascension is not a spatial movement, but the reunion of Jesus with the disciples in the Father:

'Where I am going you cannot follow me now; but you shall follow afterward' (13.36).

'I will come again and take you to myself, that where I am you may be also' (14.3).[2]

'Because I live, you will live also. In that day you will know that I am in my Father, and you in me, and I in you.' (14.19 f.).

On the Cross Jesus goes to the Father, he lives; at the Resurrection and onwards the disciples live in him and he in them. It is this mutual indwelling in love, which is the essence of the *Parousia,* and the reason therefore why in the first instance the 'manifestation' is possible only to those who love him (14. 20–3).[3]

[1]Cf. Dodd's commentary on the words, 'Do not hold me, for I have not yet ascended to the Father; but go to my brethren and say to them, I am ascending to my Father and your Father, to my God and your God' (op. cit., pp. 442 f.).

[2]This saying, it was suggested earlier (p. 25 n. 1), may be the Johannine version of 'the word of the Lord' claimed by Paul in I Thess. 4.14–17. Paul writes: 'Since we believe that Jesus died and rose again, even so through Jesus God will bring with him' both the quick and the dead, and 'we who are alive . . . shall be caught up together with them in the clouds to meet the Lord in the air; and so we shall always be with the Lord'. This is exactly what John here says in non-apocalyptic terms (cf. also 17.24; 'that they may be with me where I am, to behold my glory') and which he refers *to the Resurrection,* as already inaugurating the *Parousia.*

[3]The demurrer, 'Lord, what has happened that you will manifest yourself to us, and not to the world?' could be held to offer the sole instance (apart from the epilogue in 21.22 f.) in which John is deliberately providing a corrective to the 'traditional' *Parousia*

Here we have the complete integration of eschatology and ethics. In Matthew, the most apocalyptic of the Gospels, the division between the two is, as we saw, at its maximum. In John there are no 'ethics'. The 'new commandment', to 'love as I have loved you' (13.34), is simply the imperative of the new indicative, the *indicatio* or 'making known' by Jesus of the Father's 'name', the purpose of which is specifically 'that the love with which thou hast loved me may be in them, and I in them' (17.26). The eschatological event, the apocalypse of the name (cf. Rev. 2.17; 3.12) or final will of God, does not bring in a situation where ethics are irrelevant, as in the apocalyptic tradition, where ethics become 'interim ethics', valid only *until* the Kingdom comes. For the *Parousia* is itself the 'manifestation' or 'consummation' (I John 2.5; 4.12, 17) of love— the mutual indwelling through the Spirit of the love of the Father and of the Son and of the disciples.

This manifestation or consummation is inaugurated at the Resurrection, as the King returns to 'his own'. But it does not stop there; for there *is* to be a manifestation to the world and not only to the disciples. The unity of the disciples in the love of the Father and the Son has precisely as its end 'that the world may know that thou hast sent me' (17.21, 23; cf. 13.35). This is the Johannine equivalent of the Synoptic assurance that the End cannot come till the Gospel has been preached to the whole world (Mark 13.10; Matt. 24.14). But in John even the manifestation to the world, like everything else, is inaugurated in the Paschal events: there is nothing *merely* future. Thus in 8.28 it is said that at the lifting up of the Son of man the *Jews* (and not only the disciples, as in 16.23) will know the truth about Jesus. And the same interpretation of the Passion, as the apocalypse to the world, is also to be found in 14.30 f.,

---

expectation (in 11.21–7 the correction is of Jewish, not Christian, eschatology). But it is most naturally taken as a further expression of the attitude already reflected in 7.3–9: 'If you do these things, show yourself to the world'. For there Jesus had implied that when 'his time' *did* come, he *would* manifest himself to the world. For the fulfilment of this, see below, pp. 179 f.

if Dr Dodd's proposed punctuation (op. cit., p. 409) is accepted: 'The ruler of this world is coming. He has no claim upon me; but, *to show the world* that I love the Father and do exactly as he commands—up, let us march to meet him.'

Such is the Johannine picture. It will be seen that it does not stand alone or unsupported. On the contrary, it is clearly in basic accord with what we took to be the mind of Jesus himself, and a direct extension and deepening of the position alike of the earliest preaching and of the original Synoptic tradition. And if, indeed, it is independent of that tradition, it provides powerful support for supposing that this way of thinking was at one stage at least as widespread in the Church as later the *Parousia* doctrine was to become. But if, fundamentally, we accept its interpretation, are we then committed to writing off the whole of the other line of development as a mistake?

Misplaced expectations it certainly contains. Indeed, the very fact that the apocalyptic programme signally failed to materialize, and the expedients to which its exponents have been driven ever since, at least suggest that something may have gone wrong. The stretching of figures such as we find in II Peter 3.8 is a counsel of despair. It has always been the last refuge of apocalyptic minds: days and years can never be allowed to remain what originally they were. But the time-limit of a generation was already running out by the time that Matthew wrote; and there is no proper sense in which the modern doctrine of a second coming at an indefinitely remote time can claim to be the heir of an expectation which was nothing if it was not for the immediate future. To say that it is always 'at hand' is legitimate if one is dealing with the significance of a myth, but not if one is referring to a literal event. As such it simply did not occur.

But the mistake lay not in the very conception of a future *Parousia,* which, despite occasional crudities, represents in dramatic terms a vivid and profound picture of the summing up of all things in Christ. What went wrong was when this picture, this myth, was taken for literal event, a second event parallel with the first, lying on the same temporal line, and separated from it by an interval, whose length could be measured, 'if not now, then immediately after the second has happened'.[1]

The myth is of very real value if it enables us to see, projected and focused, as it were, in a picture of *a* 'last day', what in these 'last days' is true, through however dark a glass, of every day. For 'henceforth' we live with the Christ who comes. No less than the Jews faced by their hour of visitation, must we ever since be 'as men who wait for their master' with 'loins girded and lamps burning' (Luke 12.35 f.). For the coming of the Son of man is not merely an event of past history, finished and done with. Its tense is not simply an aorist, but a perfect. It is a visitation of God to his world, and a vindication of God to his world, by which from then on that world has been and is being confronted. *We live* in the day of the Son of man that broke first into history upon 'that generation', in a world now subject to his rule and under his judgement. That rule and that judgement are still, to be sure, merely inaugurated, and are everywhere opposed: only within the Church, as the fourth Gospel makes clear, can the *Parousia*, the presence of our returning Lord, yet be expressed in other than mythological terms. For the rest we need constantly a picture, a vision of what it must be like, of what it will be like, when 'the kingdom of the world has become the kingdom of our Lord and of his Christ' (Rev. 11.15). And to supply that vision is the indispensable function of apocalypse. For without the vision the people perish. And in the *Parousia* that vision is focused. For there, despite everything, 'we see Jesus . . . crowned with glory and honour' (Heb. 2.9) and 'the Son of man sitting at the right hand of Power, and coming with the clouds of heaven' (Mark 14.62).

That *is* the glory of this world from now on, *and* what it must become. It is this that the myth of the *Parousia* portrays, precisely as the myth of the Fall, of the first Adam, portrays

[1]Minear, *The Christian Hope and the Second Coming*, p. 75.

the world in its present wretchedness, and as it has been, go back as far as we may. Either myth loses its value when it is made to describe not what is now and persistently true, whether forwards or backwards, but a datable event, whether near or remote. In other words, the *Parousia*, or any other element in the myth of the End, becomes a distortion of the teaching of Jesus, at the point at which it is no longer a symbol, a 'sign', for the great 'henceforth' of the Gospel, but an event which cannot take place till *after* other events. And this it has clearly become both in the Pauline and Synoptic apocalypses: it cannot occur till after the great 'apostasy' (II Thess. 2.3; Mark 13.5–7) and 'the man of lawlessness is revealed' (II Thess. 2.3), till 'after the tribulation' (Mark 13.24) and 'the gospel has first been preached to all nations' (Mark 13.10). For at that point it loses its challenge as representing something that is true, and can become true, of any time and any moment from now on.[1] Eschatology is then on its way to becoming the remote appendix to Christian doctrine which it has often been, concerned with things that will happen only after everything else.

A small illustration of this process is provided by the history of a saying in the Synoptic Gospels. According to the 'Q' tradition (Matt. 10.35 f.=Luke 12.52 f.), one abiding result of the coming of Jesus will be the division of men of the same household. This is something that must ever be true, as Luke specifically says, 'from now on'. Now this feature becomes incorporated in the *Parousia* myth (Mark 13.12 and par.; Matt. 24.40 f. =Luke 17.34 f.).[2] This is entirely proper, for this is what the *Parousia* myth is meant to present—the realities of the new, the coming age. But when the myth becomes a programme, as it has done in Mark 13, then this item takes its place as one in an unfolding series of events, each of which

[1] I owe this point to a conversation with the Reverend R. F. Hettlinger, Fellow of St Augustine's College, Canterbury.

[2] It had at an earlier stage passed in a similar way from the Prophets (Mic. 7.6; Isa. 19.2; Ezek. 38.21) into Jewish apocalyptic (I Enoch 100.1 f.; II Baruch 70.3–7; IV Ezra 5.9; 6.24).

becomes valid only at a certain stage. Its power is lost, except over the curious.

Originally for the New Testament the *Parousia* language describes what is true from now on: it embraces, that is to say, *both* the finished work of Christ *and* that which has yet to be completed. But, with the disruption of this unity, it has come to refer exclusively to that half of Christian eschatology which has *not* been realized in the life, death and resurrection of Jesus. Consequently, any reappraisal of this language will always encounter the charge that this element in the Christian hope is being undermined, in the interests of a more fully 'realized' eschatology. This is, in fact, a complete misconception, though it is probably impossible to eradicate. What is at issue is not the *weight* to be allowed to the futurist element. No one can read the New Testament without constant reminder that all things are not yet in subjection (Heb. 2.8) and without hearing the cry of the saints, 'How long?' (Rev. 6.10). The coming of Christ is every bit as much future as it is past. What is at issue is the *nature* of this other half of Christian eschatology.

The answer given by the apocalyptic tradition is that it is another event, at a measurable interval from the first, for which Christians must now, and always, be skinning their eyes. But this precisely is what cannot be found in the expectation of Jesus.

The other half of Christian eschatology is not an event at all, as if another event were needed. It is, for John, the person and work of the Paraclete, who takes the things of Jesus and makes perfect in us his presence of love. It is, for the Epistle to the Hebrews, the perpetual intercession of the Priest-King, appearing henceforward within the veil on our behalf. It is, in Pauline terms, the Body of Christ, into which all is being brought, 'by that power which enables him even to subject all things to himself' (Phil. 3.21).

This 'henceforth' can indeed be represented by the myth of the *Parousia*; and none of these three writers excludes it, Paul least of all. Indeed, it occurs in the very context of the words just quoted from Philippians. Yet it is noticeable that the conception of the *Parousia* appears in the Pauline Epistles in almost inverse proportion to that of the Body of Christ. As the dangers of apocalyptic become more apparent to him, he seems to have cast round for a mode of expression that would *bring together* rather than contrast the lowly body, the self-emptying coming, of the Incarnation, and that of the *Totus Christus,* whose glory is precisely the inclusion of all in him who is the Head. It is to be observed how, right through his writings, whether in the highly mythological language of our being caught up to Christ in the air (I Thess. 4.17) or in the maturer vision of our growing up into him in all things (Eph. 4.15), Paul never ceases to present the final consummation in corporate terms (cf. I Thess. 3.13 (?), II Thess. 1.10; 2.1; Rom. 8.17–23, 29; Col. 3.4; Phil. 3.20 f.). This is why the *Parousia* and the Body of Christ can stand as theological equivalents for that eschatological reality to which the whole work of God is moving. Both represent our final 'assembling together to him' (II Thess. 2.1), our ultimate incorporation into the glory and the fulness of Christ.[1]

In this, again, Paul is close to the thinking of John, for whom the *Parousia* is essentially Christ united to his own. As a result, the eschatology of the Epistle to the Ephesians comes to be in all essentials that of the Fourth Gospel. Paul's is the theology of the 'twice-born', of the man who has been through the whole gamut of that kaleidoscopic process which marks the

[1]For further elaboration of the place occupied for Paul by the doctrine of the Body of Christ I must refer to my book, *The Body*. This concept, like the theology of Rom. 8, is an excellent example of how, even when Paul ceases to be apocalyptic in expression, he remains eschatological in his thinking. Cf. also the transition from the highly mythological and discontinuous conception of the putting on of the new being in I Cor. 15.51 f., 'We shall all be changed, in a moment, in the twinkling of an eye, at the last trumpet', to the more organic and continuous, but no less eschatological, conception of II Cor. 3.18: 'We all, with unveiled face, beholding the glory of the Lord, are being changed into his likeness from one degree of glory to another; for this comes from the Lord who is the Spirit'.

development of eschatological thinking within that fateful generation. For John the course seems to have run more calmly, in the less exposed corner of the Palestinian world in which the tradition behind the Fourth Gospel appears originally to have ripened.

But this convergence is not merely the coincidence of great minds thinking alike. For both had all the time been sharing at a much deeper level than the intellect in the same common life of the one Church, grounded in the common preaching, fed by the common sacraments. Both were one, as we are one, in the Christ who still comes, as once he came, by water and by blood (I John 5.6);[1] one in the Christ whom from the beginning the ancient '*Marana tha*' prayer (I Cor. 16.22) has invoked to stand among his own and make his real presence known. And it is in this liturgical life of the Church, in the Advent season which prepares for Christmas and the End at once, that there is still preserved at once the simplest and the most profound expression of the truth, never lost in the New Testament, that *parousia* is a word that has no plural. There is but one coming, begun at Christmas, perfected on the Cross, and continuing till all are included in it. And again, there is but one coming from God and to God. Whether ultimately we speak, with John, of Christ coming to us or, with Paul, of our coming into Christ is a matter of human language. What is decisive is that in each case we see that coming already *inaugurated,* whether in the great perfect of the Johannine 'It is finished' (John 19.30) or in that tremendous aorist in which the Apostle to the gentiles declares (Eph. 1.10) that it was the design of God, once and for all, in the fulness of time, 'to sum up all things' in Christ.

[1]The primary reference of this verse is to the Incarnation. Jesus is the Christ by virtue of his baptism *and* his death: the divine Christ did not leave the human Jesus before the Crucifixion, as the Docetists asserted. But there is almost certainly a reference also to the manner in which the Christ comes to the believer now, in the Spirit, by Baptism and the Eucharist.

INDEX OF NAMES

INDEX OF SCRIPTURAL PASSAGES